REVIEV

-"Like a witty friend, with strength and full of common sense."

Dr. Cesar Fermin, Professor and Dean
Tuskegee University, Retired

-"Smart, tart and full of heart."

Michele Finley, BSCE
Author of Children's Books

-"Cody Wayne Foote has done something remarkable by sharing a host of his original thoughts, sayings and humorous anecdotes not just with his family and friends, but with everybody. I'm glad he chose to share them with me. It is a fun read, almost like Proverbs with a lot of humor added."

Reverend Dr. James Bankhead
Presbyterian Minister, Retired

LIMERICKS,
LIES
and
LUNACY

LIMERICKS,
LIES
and
LUNACY

Cody Wayne Foote

Xulon Press

Xulon Press
2301 Lucien Way #415
Maitland, FL 32751
407.339.4217
www.xulonpress.com

Printed in the United States of America.

ISBN-13: 978-1-6322-1558-1

PREFACE

To the Reader: This book gives you a subtle road map to a successful life, for love and happiness, and just like Mama's "biscuits" are made with an ounce of humor, a dash of spirituality, a sprinkle of witticism, a spoonful of poetry, a pound of prose and a lot of love, Served up in a tantalizing and sneaky way.

For many years, I have had the fortunate or unfortunate experience of randomly having thoughts come through my head in the nature of a joke, a banter, a pun, a witticism, a proverb, a parable, and for a few seconds I enjoyed them, and if someone was close by, I would tell it to them. And, if no one was around, in just a few seconds it was gone. There were hundreds, if not thousands of them.

A few people who heard me tell them, asked me where they came from, and since I didn't really know, I would just tell them that I hear voices. Of course, I would get strange looks and thereafter those folks always put some distance between me and them. Starting a few years ago, when those thoughts would come to me, if I could, I would write them down and that is where this book came from, thoughts straight out of my crazy head.

My Wife may have an eye problem as a result of this book, because every time I thought of what I believed to be a good witticism, I would tell to her, and she would roll those eyes. And after several thousand, I think it has affected her eyes-so my apologies to her.

So, other than her, I have consulted with no one on this book, so I have to take all the criticism and, the voices get all the credit. Note: I deliberately inserted a few mistakes to keep you awake, looking for them, while reading.

1

THE GIFT OF TIME

I see and hear you my friend,

I see you struggling with life,

I want to comfort you,

But I am struggling with my own strife.

Maybe I could just stay and listen,

Though I have nothing to say,

Maybe just being there as a friend,

Can be a help in its own way,

To the disappoints of the heart,

To the stress of the mind

It may be the best a friend can do,

Is the giving of their limited time.

We walk through life's path,

Carrying heavy burdens down the road,

But, walking with a friend who listens,

Will lift and lighten the load.

We will never really know

The inner stress and anxiety of another,

But we, if nothing else, can be there

And offer a shoulder like a brother.

I don't really know much about,

Complex situations and such,

But I can be quiet and listen,

I know that I can do that much.

If you need me my friend,

Just call on me anytime,

And your worries, and your burdens,

Will also be mine.

As with our children and our friends,

Our greatest gift and one sublime,

Is just being there and listening,

And giving of our precious time.

Love is not an accident.

Real love asks for nothing in return.

It's hard to be happy by yourself, probably means, it was meant to be shared.

Don't be caught doing stinking thinking, or you may be sinking to where the police lights are blinking.

Think while you are moving, because if you stop to think, you get behind in the race.

Many small successes can add up to a really big win.

Taking a pause is not the same as quitting.

Old asphalt workers never die, they just pave the way.

Feeling is not always done by the hands.

Never substitute dreams for hope, and never substitute hope for work.

Claude: You once said I would make a good husband, what changed your mind?

Maude: I married you.

You show character by asking, not assuming.

The right time, will, in time, present itself.

The secret to a full life is to never leave behind unused potential.

2

I WORK

I work for necessities of life,

I work for a reason and purpose for life,

I work for the fulfillment of life,

I work to have valuable goals in life,

I work to give back to life,

I work for the joy of doing in life,

I work because work solves problems in life,

I work because work extends life,

I work because I enjoy life,

I work because work is life.

If a man doesn't plan for tomorrow today, he needs to learn to like surprises.

How to keep a woman happy –every day tell her you love her and every day tell your sorry—for what? Doesn't matter, if you haven't done something to be sorry for by the time you tell her you love her, you probably will before the day is done.

Have your brain running before you shift your mouth into gear.

Every life is filled with rain, but after every rain there is a rainbow.

First moron: You say you don't understand women, why is that?

Second moron: Every time I tell my girl I love her she cries.

No need to look for trouble, it will find you.

No wonder there are no chairs, everyone is always being directed to take a seat.

I don't hate anybody, but I have good reasons to strongly dislike a lot of them.

First moron: Do you feel sorry for robbing the bank?

Second moron: I did until I counted the money.

I wonder what God thinks about political correctness.

The meek shall inherit the earth, but I want a little bit more than dirt.

Maude: My mother told me about men like you.

Claude: After five husbands, she ought to know.

Old night people never die, they just wait for the mourning.

With enough polish, every gem will shine.

In many things in life, down is easy, up is hard.

You don't have to be on a different planet to be a world apart.

3

WHEN YOU KNOW IT

If you didn't know it before you knew you didn't know that you didn't know that you didn't know that you didn't know it, then you probably won't know it after you know you don't know that you don't know it.

If you want to get better, always compete with someone who is better than you.

You don't have to be rich or famous to have honor.

With sex, any more than you can stand means you may have to lie down.

There are very few pickpockets with big hands.

These days it's really depressing how many people are suffering from depression.

Don't spread gossip, enjoy it all by yourself.

Claude: My mother said you were a tramp.

Maude: Your mother would know.

Heaven is just one breath away and so is hell.

They say that truth is stranger than lies, not so, they have not heard the ones I tell.

There are some people who seem to have great experience at kneeling.

First moron: Your brother thought he was a horse so you entered him into a derby?

Second moron: Yeah-he came in second place, and we needed the money.

How many days of a man's life will he have to be reminded to take out the garbage without being asked—all of them.

How to make the marriage alive with new things is by making many things unpredictable into predictable and many things predictable into unpredictable, but it will be rough for a while.

The road to heaven is rough and dangerous.

The road to hell is deceptively smooth.

Nobody is too small to not do something really big.

Perhaps the loudest sound we will ever hear are the whispered words I love you.

Do the right thing because you care, not because you might be rewarded.

There is a number lonelier than one-zero.

If the road you're on is leading to a bad end, use a different road, even if you have to build one.

Almost everyone who asks for help will get it-it's the human way.

Old sick debtors never die, they just cough it up.

Teachers do it in front of the class.

It's not about winning, it's about how you play the game is what you tell yourself when you don't win first place, never when you win first place.

Remember the way to Heaven is up.

Your brain is wrong 50% of the time, and your feeling are wrong 50% of the time-good luck.

Never underestimate the power of stupidity.

Make one new friend each day, for you never know when you are going to need one.

You may have an ugly face, but a personality so beautiful that nobody notices your face.

If all you do is look for faults, you will find every one of them.

If you never help anyone, don't be surprised that no one wants to help you.

If you get to Heaven before me, try to save a place for me, and if you can, put in a good word for me.

Always keep one eye searching for the good and one eye watching for the bad.

Claude: I'm going to Hawaii on my vacation this year, where are you going?

Maude: To see a lawyer.

Leaving is easy, coming back is hard, especially after everybody tells everything they know about you while you are gone.

They say a fool and his money soon part-now you know why I hang out with the people I do.

When it comes to sex, even an amateur can be an expert.

4

THE WEATHER

When the weather is hot,

Bemoan it not,

When the weather is cold,

Put it on hold,

When the weather is in-between,

Dance and sing.

Many people live an entire life and never know why.

Good little boys go to heaven, bad little boys go everywhere but heaven.

Always have some truth in your lies, just in case you get caught.

Sometimes the naked truth needs some clothes.

There is little time if you're going to say you're sorry, so say it now.

If I knew then what I don't know now, I would know the answer before I know the question.

When you have a burning desire, it's hard to put out the flames.

First moron: Know how to stop a bully?

Second moron: Yes, with a bigger bully.

I don't lie, I just give the truth some depth.

Money won't get you into heaven, but it can get you to the door.

If it's true as they say our feet continue to grow, then our mouth should grow correspondingly for obvious reasons.

As in travel, as in life, the road you choose will determine your destination.

The problem with masturbation is, you have to do it all by yourself.

It's just as important for one to be as good a steward with his life as with his money.

Wasted time is wasted life.

Nobody is given extra time to make things right, so do it in the time you have.

The general rule doesn't necessarily apply to everybody.

Looking out is always easier than looking in.

Sometimes no is the answer whether you take it or not.

Maude: Why do you always come home drunk?

Claude: It's the only way I can come home.

Can't treat all people as human, because some of them aren't.

Old bullies never die, they just get full of bull.

A coward already has one enemy before he is attacked.

Athletes do it in their jockey shorts.

Old lawyers never die, and that is just contemptable.

Maude: My mother warned me about men like you.

Claude: Did she warn you about men not like me?

To feel love, you must feel with your heart, to understand love, you must see it with your mind.

They said go West young man, I would but I'm not a young man anymore.

Learn and do as much as you can, so when older, life doesn't end before you.

The human touch keeps us in touch with humanity.

The generations before us left us many great things, cars, airplanes, medicine, psychology, what are you leaving for the next generation?

Repeating a lie many times may make you want to believe it, but that does not make it true.

The problem with communism and socialism is they disincentivise one to excel, and punishes one who does.

I'd rather have people wonder why I don't speak than why I do.

One day the common ground will be controlled by the common man, in an uncommon way.

The world I see is colored by me.

5

CHOICES

What we have in a free society, more than anything, is choices. If you don't like where you live, then move. If you don't like your job, get another one. If you don't like your friends, get some new ones. If you don't make as much money as you would like, get more education and skills and get a better job. Even if you don't like yourself, you can, with effort change, it's tough, but you can change. Anything you don't like, you can change.

Many people live unhappy lives because they make bad choices, and the crazy thing is they keep making them over and over and it becomes a habit which is hard to break, but all the while, expecting a different result each time. Habits are good indicators of a successful life or a failed one. If you want a happy, successful life, make good choices and make them so much, they become life's best choice habit.

If you have feelings that you need to show and tell, do it now for tomorrow you may not get the chance.

First moron: You say your wife doesn't want sex anymore, how do you know?

Second moron: I overheard her tell her sister on a phone call.

If wishing really worked, we would all be billionaires by now.

If marriages are made in heaven, why do so many end up in hell?

Hope keeps dreams alive.

To climb the ladder of success, first learn how to build a ladder.

If a man asks you for a dollar give it to him, if he ask for $20, have him sign a promissory note.

They say reach for the stars, but it's a good thing they are far away, because they do get a little hot.

Think of God above and show a little love.

Guard your secrets carefully, in the hands of your enemies they are powerful weapons.

Claude: You sure do have a big butt.

Maude: Yeah, about the size of your mouth, so how about a kiss.

Old glue makers never die, they just stick with it.

Lovers do it between the sheets.

People who look down on others are usually stuck-up.

That's the way it goes, first your money, then your clothes.

If you could see the world through my eyes, you would see beauty beyond words.

I wish I could absorb all the hate in the world and jump in the ocean and take it with me.

There are two types of people, those who build and those who tear down, which are you?

And it all came down to just you, and you have the only key.

This is a land of fishermen, everybody is fishing for something, money, fame, friends, love, salvation, opportunity, entertainment, forgiveness, peace, and a few who are actually fishing for fish, and to all of you fishermen, may your net always be more than one-half full.

The whole world may not be upside down, it may be just you.

You could develop a psychosis worrying about all the people who are psychotic.

As a matter of fact, it is a factual matter that there is no fact without matter and matter without fact, and in short, facts matter.

My getting serious usually becomes a laughing matter.

Nobody can be you better than you.

It's hard to live a purposeful life if you don't know its purpose.

Sex can be in the genes, but it is better naked.

Claude: I'll hold your hands so I can relax.

Maude: No, I'll hold your hands so I can relax.

Ballet dancers do it in their tights.

If you can convince the world that you really mean it when you say you would die for freedom then maybe you won't have to.

They say only people can make you ecstatically happy and ragingly unhappy, but the truth is people only give us a rational excuse to feel one way or the other. We ourselves hold the key to feel which way.

6

YOUR SOLUTION

Your solution to you is you. Nobody knows more about you than you, nobody knows more about your fears than you, nobody knows more about your strengths and weaknesses than you, nobody knows more about your goals and aspirations than you, nobody knows more about your feelings than you. The problem is we plan, execute those plans, and judge ourselves by what we think others expect of us, and, what we wish we were rather than who we are. You already more about yourself than anybody, and you really know what you can do, so, just go ahead and do your best at what you do best. You are the solution to you.

If someone tells you they have no secrets, they have lived a very dull life.

If you have a story to tell, tell it, it may be just what someone needs to hear.

What do you call a conceited person who has no qualities justifying being conceited—an ass.

Marriage must be contagious every time a man gets married so does a woman.

Pray, it's later than you think.

Not everything not true is also false.

Money is not evil, it's the people who have it.

First moron: They say there's nothing to fear but fear itself.

Second moron: You have just added another one to my list.

Pilots do it in high places.

Old tire makers never die, they just keep treading along.

They say there are no free lunches, and that probably includes breakfast and dinner.

Work for, hope and believe that good will triumph over evil. What other choice do you have?

Just so you will know, you don't have to have a knife to cut the mustard.

The dishonest person has more to answer to than the police; ultimately he will have to answer to himself.

We sing, same old song, second verse, probably because it's the only song we know, and can't remember the first verse.

Maude: I want to tell you a secret.

Claude: If you tell me, then it won't be a secret.

Don't tell me everything you don't know, I'm only here for one life-time.

Jesus said we would always have the poor with us, but that was before welfare.

Old secretaries never die, they just keep making copies.

7

WHAT I SEE

Come listen to the waggle, said the tongue to the ear,

There will be things you'll learn and things you don't want to hear,

And, you'll learn much of friends, many things of your foe,

Some things will be good, and many things you don't want to know.

For, if we look deep inside, to see who we are and who we can be,

You'll see many things good, but, many of them you don't want to see,

You'll see secrets down there, where it gets dark down that deep,

Some of them you will regret, and some of them you will keep.

Some of them will be friends and some of them will not,

And, you'll notice something strange, the distance between is not a lot,

Foes will carelessly do good and friends will carelessly do bad,

And seeing these role reversals can sometimes make you sad.

Sometimes we identify with the foe, and sometimes with the friend,

Roles change, become reversed and are right back at the beginning again,

Now the picture becomes cloudy, we no longer can see enough to tell,

With moving targets, which one is Heaven and which one is Hell.

But still, both the friend and the foe, we regretfully can very well see,

Because, for whatever reason, they both look exactly like me.

Old summer mountain climbers never die, they just keep waiting for the fall.

Old gossipers never die, they just get promoted to manure spreaders.

Maude: I don't see how we can make this work out.

Claude: I know a Judge who can.

If everything were done halfway where would we all be.

How many red-necks does it take to make moonshine—one, if he's sober.

If there were a supernatural data storage that had all the answers to every possible question in the universe and you had access to it how much of it would you want to know?

If in life, while chasing your dreams, you find something good, grab it and hold on as long as you have breath.

Old used car salesman never die, they just sale away.

Many people are waiting for the magic day-every day is magic, and you are the magician.

Everybody can do good, how much effort does it take to keep your mouth shut.

Old boxers never die, they just knock a round.

Just so you will know, everybody does not necessarily include you.

The lay of the land is not a place where you sleep.

One too many always sinks the boat.

Just because a man is down, does not necessarily mean he is out, he through perseverance and hard work can rise and be stronger than he was before.

If you have to go in circles, at least make the circle as big as possible.

I dream, I wonder, I think, I believe, I do, or, I don't dream, I don't wonder, I don't think, I don't believe, and I don't do. Now you know the process.

Whatever good you can do is what you should do.

You don't have to build a road every time you want to go somewhere, take advantage of what's available.

You show your character every time you show good manners and every time you don't.

Claude: What do you like about me?

Maude: Not a damn thing.

You can never be wrong by being polite.

Bakers do it in the oven.

Old historians never die, they just stay in the past.

The most crucial measurement we ever make is the margin of error.

8

UNFIT

I went to the doctor for a checkup like I knew I should,

He looked, listened, poked and said my health was not good,

He gave me a prognosis of wrong and mostly it was too fat,

And summed it all up by saying I was un-fit at that.

He said go to the gym and exercise and pump some steel,

And, get on a cycle and push and peddle and spin the wheel,

Go on a diet, cut down on the food, the calories and the fat,

Get down on all fours and crawl and scurry around like a rat.

No junk food, no fast food, not anything that's good to eat,

And, definitely no candy, no deserts and nothing that's sweet,

After weeks of hunger and starving right down to my soul,

I was at the same 207, and down to dry rice in a small bowl.

But, the weight remained and hung on like it was stuck with glue,

And, I ate super health foods that smelled and tasted like poo,

So, I looked and asked everyone every way I would turn,

Please help me, I need help, I have a million calories to burn.

Most ideas were a sort of home remedy only a fool would try,

I was about ready to jump up and down and scream and cry,

So, I have come to accept what the doctor said , I am un-fit,

And, I am upset, disturbed and don't like it one little bit.

So, I started wearing oversized clothes that didn't fit,

And did all I could to hide my fat, and in doing, used all my wit,

And then a soldier told me about the best idea I have heard yet,

Join the Army, and they will shape you up on that you can bet.

So, I went down to the recruiter and signed on the dotted line,

And, agreed to be an enlistee in the Army and do my time,

Off to basic training with everybody running to and fro,

Running everywhere whenever and wherever we would go.

We did exercise, PT, which I believe stands for permanent terror,

And, for food, they call chow, was something that was a horror,

After weeks of this, the drill sergeant said we had to weigh in,

So, one by one we stepped on his scales, and he called out the trend.

I was hoping my weight was down, after and through what I had been,

I had weighed in at 207, so I was expecting it to be down by eleven,

I could not believe my eyes at the numbers I saw on those scales,

And, was in stark disbelief when I looked at the scales and saw 207.

The drill sergeant growled and was not happy, not one little bit,

He yelled and cussed and said I was not only unfit, but also a misfit,

I'll get that weight down I tell you, if it's the last thing I ever do,

I've got an outfit that will fit you just right, that's where I sending you.

So, he sent me to a group of misfits that were named the misfit unfit,

I had a new uniform, a blue, that said I was in the misfit unfit outfit,

We worked harder than before, they got our sweat, every little bit,

If I was going to lose all that weight, it was here I would lose it.

So, I doubled down, and worked longer and harder then before,

And, it got to the point I could hardly take it and go on any more,

The Captain came to check and look over this outfit of unfit and misfit,

He stopped and said to me, those clothes are ill fitting and don't fit.

So, I turned in my uniform which was made for the big and tall,

And, was given one that was too short, too little and too small,

When I complained about the size, they laughed fit to be tied,

And, about the uniform, I was a trouble maker and had lied.

The drill sergeant put me on the scales to see if I am now fit,

Your weight is still 207 and it is not down, not one little bit,

There is just one more thing I can think of I can do,

I'll send you on maneuvers, and that will be good for you.

They said we were going on maneuvers and gave me one-half a tent.

I understood the shovel, and its use, but not what the other meant.

We walked for hours on a narrow road that crooked and bent,

And, I spent an hour trying figure out the puzzle of the tent.

They told us to find another person with which our one-half was to fit,

I looked and asked and got no one, so my one-half, I was stuck with it

During the night the rain and the cold came, I got sick, and I was down,

The captain said take me to the hospital and the first doctor found.

The doctor checked my vitals, put me on his scale to check my weight,

He read my weight and looked at my chart and said this can't wait,

You're down 57 pounds, you are anemic, and unfit for this outfit,

I'm unfit to fit with the unfit outfit of misfits with a uniform misfit.

But I'm happy to know I'm fit and no longer unfit or extra-large,

I'm also happy to know I going to get an army medical discharge,

So, now I receive a monthly check for being a soldier who is unfit,

Even though I am the most fit and fitted unfit soldier to be fitted for a fit.

I can't explain it any other way, it must have been a piece of Heaven,

That those scales in the drill sergeant's office was stuck on 207.

Being conceited is not so bad as long as you're not arrogant about it.

It's amazing how many problems between men and women get solved quickly with a diamond.

Dumb: I thought you were going to start a mechanic on wheels business.

Dumber: I am as soon as I can get somebody to help me crank my truck.

Don't trust your illusions they are all probably just delusions.

Just because I can't see what you see does not mean I can't appreciate that you can.

You have to work at love for love to work.

9

WISHING TO WHATEVER

I wish I could, Is replaced with

I think I can, Is replaced with

I am sure I can, Is replaced with

I know I can, Is replaced with

Without a doubt I can, Is replaced with

Whatever it takes.

Maude: You have wasted all our money on wine, women and song, what do you have to say for yourself?

Claude: You told me to start acting like an adult.

There is gold in them there hills, if you don't believe it check with one of the ladies who walk the streets of Beverly Hills.

No matter who you are, where you come from, what you believe, if you could see the world through my eyes, you might have a different point of view.

Dumb: Do you know the secret to a long life?

Dumber: Yes, don't die

Everything begins with attitude, because attitude becomes a pattern of thinking and that pattern becomes a habit that shapes your mood and your behavior, so if there is anything about yourself you want to change, hopefully for the better, start with your attitude.

Hate and love cannot co-exist, either love will conquer hate, or hate will consume love.

To my ex-wife, I can't give you anything but love, you took all the rest.

Maude: We will grow old together.

Claude: Well, you are one-half right.

Old alcoholics never die, because they are 90 proof.

Fortunately, the system is rigged, God has a plan for our salvation even though no one deserves it.

Cowboys do it in their boots.

Dumb: You say you had a shotgun wedding, who held the gun, her Dad?

Dumber: No, she did.

You never get a second chance to be the first one to show love, kindness, understanding or patience.

When love dies, it goes back to God where it came from, to be held in reserve for the next person who needs it and will use it.

To get rid of stress do these four steps 1. Smile, 2. Laugh, 3. Cry, 4. Laugh again and repeat as often as necessary.

10

YOUR FRIEND

I can't make your life easy,

Nor, stop it from being queasy,

I can't make you a star,

Only help you be who you are.

I can't make you smart,

Or, be something your aren't,

I can't make others respect you,

But, I can show you I do.

I can't stop your pain,

Nor, keep it from coming again,

I can't help you find love,

Even if that's what you're thinking of.

I can't give you a better life,

Or, even remove its strife,

But, one thing I can do to the end,

Is, forever be your friend.

Just because somethings are out of sight and out of reach does not mean they're unobtainable.

If it is too good to be true, it usually is.

If you are waiting on others to help you attain your goals, you may be waiting a long time.

If you believe, really, really believe something will happen, it's amazing how often it does.

If you had the tenacity and persistence of a thirsty gnat around the eye of the South Floridian in August you could accomplish almost anything.

Never ask for help if you don't really need it, because every time you do, you become one step weaker.

Maude: If you made a lot of money, we would be rich.

Claude: No I'd be rich and you'd be single.

I'm not procrastinating; I'm just giving the world one more chance.

If you hate yourself whether you admit it or not you'll never be at peace.

An act of kindness works both ways.

If we live in a selfish world as we are constantly told, why then, after we do a selfless act of kindness do we feel so good.

Old rich people never die, it just wouldn't be profitable.

11

WHAT I BELIEVE

I believe in God, a Supreme Creator, salvation through redemption of sins, and therefore I believe there is a reason for our existence, a purpose for every person.

I believe in the family, the character of men and the strength of a nation is determined by the family unit, and countries that do not protect the family will fail.

I believe in the United States of America, for what it has done, is doing, and will do for me, my family and friends, and I owe my full and unending allegiance to it.

I believe in the people of the United States of America, for their unbelievably big heart, for their universal desire to help the underdog, the less fortunate, the oppressed and the helpless.

I believe in freedom, not just as an idea, but as a working goal to be pursued and relentlessly, both individually and collectively, it is the God ordained destiny for every person and every nation, that it is worth dying for, and therefore worth living for, and once attained is meant to be given away.

I believe in the Constitution of the United States, and not just as a revered parchment, but as a living, working guide for the government and the people.

I believe in Individual Initiative, that one person, one vote and one life can make a difference in the world.

I believe in Loyalty, that it is not an outdated idea, and I believe in being loyal to one's family, one's friends, one's country and one's own beliefs.

I believe in hard work, that personal achievement and satisfaction come from hard work, that a country's national pride in itself is improved through hard work, and hard work builds the character of a person and a nation.

I believe in the spirit of compromise, that it is in this way that men and nations achieve the most for the common good, but compromise should never be the lazy path that leads to loss of Liberty.

I believe in myself, that I can make a difference, that if I apply myself through hard work, using my mental and physical abilities, I can do worthwhile things for myself, my family, my country, and the common good.

I believe in aspiring to and reaching new goals for myself, my country and the world, and dreaming of a better world is a common theme for all men and all nations, and through diligence, hard work, and compromise, such a better world is within our reach.

Smile at your enemies, it will confuse them and give you the upper hand.

Happiness will come to those who eagerly search for it.

Dumb: How far away is Heaven and Hell?

Dumber: About the same distance, it takes one lifetime to get to either place.

You know times are really tough when all the atheists have begun to pray

I'm waiting on patience, but not for long.

Sex makes the body produce a lot of dopamine with emphasis on the dope part.

This war between the sexes, I'm not going to take it lying down.

You will never get to the bottom of things, if you always believe you are on top.

Dumb: My girlfriend wants to sell pictures of her naked figure, but doesn't know how.

Dumber: She'll figure it out.

One good thing about being on the dark side of the truth is you can always say there is a brighter side.

First moron: The new generation is lazy and stupid.

Second moron: Yeah-like father like son.

I am becoming the person I chose to be because it is my choice and I am the only thing in my way.

Of all the good things that prayer does, the most immediate is on the one praying.

Sometimes love is a swell event.

Some days are an uphill battle and some days are a downhill battle.

You can't climb the ladder of success by pulling others down, the best way to climb the ladder of success is to take others with you on your way up.

12

THEY SAID

They said I should see the world as a child,

I did, then they said I was childish.

They said I should forgive and forget,

I did, but they most definitely did not.

They said I should live like there was no tomorrow,

I did, then unfortunately came tomorrow.

They said give it your all,

I did, and couldn't get it back.

They said forget about your worries and woes,

I did, but they surely didn't.

They said be kind and be patient,

I did, but they certainly weren't.

They said just do the right thing,

I did, but they disagreed with what was right.

They said I should work hard and be thrifty,

I did, and they said I was a miser.

They said I should give generously,

I did, and they took it all, every bit.

They said work hard and be good,

I did, but they didn't work or be good.

They said give your time and help others,

I did, but they never did either.

They said I should choose right over wrong,

I chose right, but they chose wrong.

They said reach out and touch someone,

I did, and was arrested for assault.

They said don't go away mad,

I went away, and they got mad.

They said to love everybody,

I tried, and got beat up many times.

They said my un-happiness was my own fault,

I just didn't follow directions.

One thing you should give up, is giving up.

My life has been and always will be a work in progress.

You grow in character twice as much as you give of yourself.

When the final bell is about to ring, grab the clapper, and hold on, hold on, hold on.

Never mistake pity for real love, on the surface they sometimes look the same.

Living on the edge can be precipitous.

The arrogant fighter's arrogance will be his downfall long term, but be ready for a deadly fight in the short-term.

One of the most exasperating things you can have is a spot that itches, that you can't quite reach, and one of the most satisfying things is when you finally reach that spot.

First moron: Who's got the biggest mouth, Democrats or Republicans?

Second moron: Republicans, however big the Democratic lie is the Republicans always swallow it.

Maude: You are so un-predictable, will you ever change?

Claude: Yes.

Old disillusioned people will never die, they just don't see it.

Sometimes you have to put things off, to keep from procrastinating.

13

THE LITTLE THINGS

It's the little things that can turn things around,

It's the little things that can makes the world go around,

It's the little things that can make a picture a work of art,

It's the little things that can make music into a symphony,

It's the little things that can make failure into a success,

It's the little things that changes fondness into love,

It's the little things that can make a good marriage great,

It's the little things that changes dark to light,

It's the little things that changes despair into hope,

It's the little things that make life worth living,

It's the little things that God gives us every day,

Thank God for the little things.

Dumb: They say he who hesitates is lost.

Dumber: Probably should be he who is lost must hesitate.

Old red bugs never die, they just get ticked off.

I will fall, you will fall, everybody will fall at some point, the question is, how soon will we get up.

Because people and things change, always have a backup for your backup for your plan to success.

Give your enemy your ear, and he may give you his heart.

Claude: Why can't I be king in my own house?

Maude: You can, as soon as you finish the dishes, mop the kitchen, and make the beds.

We need to do several extra good deeds everyday just to make up for all the thoughtless stupid things we say and do every day whether we intended to do them or not.

Promising to love more, if sincere, is itself an act of love.

Old debtors never die, they just go for broke.

Always have at least 5 hip-pocket jokes that are really funny, that you can tell anywhere, any time, and use one or more when you are in an awkward situation, and you need some pleasant distraction to disarm everybody until you get your wits together. Good advice for anybody.

Don't make yourself small by trying to be a big shot.

If, I only had one thing to say, I'm not sure I have the words to say it.

A follower follows because he does not know where he is going, so never follow a follower.

Putting things behind you leaves no room behind you to back up if such be needed.

14

WHY YOU WILL WIN

It sounded so simple when he said his request, I want to do well and be my very best. But, wanting and wishing signifies he is a spectator, not a participant. We want to excel and be recognized, but no one is going to push us into the race, and no one is going to absorb our pain throughout the grueling race and no one is going to drag us across the finish line.

There are no shortcuts to success in the race of life, there is only hard work. No one was meant to be a failure, and that's why there are so many ways to be a success, but only two ways to be a failure, either you didn't enter the race or you gave up too soon.

You don't have to come in first in every race, just finishing the race is also success. And, we all don't start at the same point, because some people are born in circumstances which give them a head start in the race and in life. But the head start was given to them. By the time you reach the place where they started from, you have become a seasoned campaigner, a road warrior, toughened by the rigors of the race, more prepared to endure the obstacles you will face.

The person who had the initial advantage may win the first race, but there are many races in life. You have to work harder and longer because of the disadvantages, but you will get stronger, more disciplined and more determined. So now in the many races to come, who has the advantage? But don't expect the person with the advantages to give up easily, he is accustomed to winning, has too much pride to lose, but hard work and determination will equal that advantage and perhaps more.

Many people who would otherwise be a success don't because it is easier to make excuses than run the race. It doesn't make any difference what the excuse is, it may sound noble or may be simple, they all have the same effect, they keep you out of the race, and you can't win if you don't run in the race. And if you are not in the race, what is your excuse.

Strippers do it naked.

In life the only straight line is down.

I tried to put it all together, but it appears someone has mixed the puzzles.

I don't want much in life just all of mine and a little of yours.

Claude: Hold me and cuddle me like a baby.

Maude: I'll hold you, but I ain't changing your diapers.

As long as there is hope there is a reason, and as long as there is a reason, there is hope.

Morning prayer: Lord help us to do all we can do, be all we can be and forgive us when we don't.

Old meek people never die, they just gain some ground.

Claude: My mother says she is a lot smarter than you.

Maude: She may right, she didn't marry you.

You may have to run the entire race, because life will not meet you half-way.

15

WHILE I WAS SLEEPING

While I was sleeping, the earth was turning and a new day will soon come,

While I was sleeping, someone dreamed about a new life,

While I was sleeping, someone had a scary nightmare,

While I was sleeping, planes flew overhead carrying thousands of people,

While I was sleeping, people in faraway places were waging war,

While I was sleeping, a mother breast-fed her baby,

While I was sleeping, a young girl practiced her ballet steps,

While I was sleeping, a young boy read about his baseball hero,

While I was sleeping, a criminal was breaking into a home,

While I was sleeping, politicians were plotting how to take more control of my life,

While I was sleeping, a young man kissed a young girl beneath a full moon,

While I was sleeping, tired old men gambled in a poorly lit backroom,

While I was sleeping, stockroom boys stocked shelves with produce for the next day,

While I was sleeping, police were making their rounds in the rough neighborhoods,

While I was sleeping, truckers were logging in the miles hauling goods,

While I was sleeping, a man told his wife he loved her and meant it,

While I was sleeping, a homeless man dreamed of a home and a warm bed,

While I was sleeping, two young children huddled together, while their single mom worked,

While I was sleeping, earthquakes and volcanoes erupted somewhere in the world,

While I was sleeping, a disturbed and angry man abused his terrified wife,

While I was sleeping, volunteers worked all night preparing food for the hungry,

While I was sleeping, a young girl cries because her mom and dad are not together,

While I was sleeping, sleepy-eyed workers were repairing the street,

While I was sleeping, a student assesses his finances for tuition money,

While I was sleeping, a young student gave her piano recital,

While I was sleeping, scientists worked on life saving new medicines,

While I was sleeping, friends and relatives were visiting a sick person in the hospital,

While I was sleeping, a man and a woman in some place were getting married, While I was sleeping, many happy students were attending their graduation,

While I was sleeping, a love struck young man proposes to his girlfriend,

While I was sleeping, I dreamed of distressing things and things of great joy,

While I was sleeping, there was darkness because there's no sunshine at night,

While I was sleeping, good and bad things happened, but the good outweighed the bad,

While I was sleeping, life continued in the night and made ready for one more day,

While I was sleeping, many looked for the coming day, and waited for it to dawn,

While I was sleeping, people were praying for a great new day,

While I was sleeping, people were hoping for a better world,

While I was sleeping, God watched over the universe, the earth and us,

As I awake, my prayer is that the light of day will bring much joy your way.

Swimmers do it in the pool.

I have news for you pessimists, rain is not the norm.

Many a selfish person has looked into his soul and found nothing.

16

WASTING TIME

People hate waiting, believing it to be a waste of time, but is it? Use it as a time to re-group, reflect on the past, plan for the future, rejuvenate yourself, renew your resolve, put power in your purpose, put faith in your hope, and your dreams into expectations, -and here you thought you were just wasting time, besides if you're only hanging around waiting, put that time to use, rather than standing around griping and bitching.

You're welcome.

Take it one day at a time is now down to take it one minute at a time

Some people are like uranium-they have a half-life.

Sometimes silence is the best answer, and sometimes it's the only answer.

They say good things come to those who wait, more likely, good things come to those who go out and get them.

Sometimes snakes come on two legs.

Some days, no matter what we do, things just seem to work out OK. Take it, accept it, and just go with the flow.

Remember stand tall, except on a battlefield.

Never listen to a financial advisor who is not rich.

First Moron: I can do almost anything.

Second Moron: Oh yeah, then find the end of a circle

I don't always know what to say but that does not stop me from saying it anyway.

Love should always be bursting at the seams.

Maude: Why do you always sleep facing the wall?

Claude: The wall doesn't talk, snore or complain.

Before you go along to get along, find out the destination of the trip.

They say don't be a sore loser-What, do they expect you to be happy about it?

Soldiers do it in their fatigues.

A good excuse is better than nothing.

You already know the answer before you hear the question, it was somebody else's fault.

Money can buy you all the sex you can stand, but not love.

Do things that make you want to love yourself, and others will too.

Florist do it in a pot.

Old writers never die, they haven't figured out an ending.

Forcing people to be equal means bringing some down.

17

THE PATIENT WIFE

You go, and here alone, I will stay,

I'll hold the fort while you blaze your way,

I will preserve, guard and I will protect,

While blazes of glory you can go and trek.

Assuming I am weaker, then here I will stay,

And hold things together and keep them that way,

As things begin to change, I will try to keep them the same,

As you go forth, travel and build your fame.

So, here is where I will stay, and here I must be,

And, winsome and lonely, there will be no fame for me,

For fame is built not on things that you've already got,

But, on promises, new ideas and things you had not.

Those who seek to build and grow a new name,

Put their name in lights and establish their fame,

And, they know very well that their name,

Will never be glorified, by keeping things the same.

So, here they go up and over new terrain,

While doing good, but always building their name,

Here I stay, quite, in the shadows where feelings I hide,

And, withdraw into myself and swallow my pride.

Sometimes I have a great and present fear,

That your search for fame will not let you come back here,

In my quiet moments I think of the times we had,

And, recount that even the worst times really weren't bad.

I wonder whether or not I can hold on this way,

Never knowing if or when you will return some day,

But I try to be positive, and to have courage, also to pray,

That I'll have that courage to hold and to hold on to that day.

Often I wonder what the world is doing to you,

Taking its pound of flesh which you obviously knew,

I have doubts, yet knowing in my heart that you are alive,

That you have the might that makes a right to survive.

As time goes on and on, I feel old and all alone,

I immediately rebound, for I won't survive with such a tone,

Time changes everything, we know that to be true,

But, I must hold on and remain the same if only for you.

So, in the future, if and when, someday you return,

You won't have a new person to watch and learn,

So then, I'll sacrifice my own desire to grow,

And, keep me much the same, this I know.

So, I wonder, I dream, pray and wait,

Then, one day there you are at the front gate,

The world has taken its toll, I can see it in his face,

What the world has taken from him, it has put age in its place.

I run to him, to hold him, and welcome him home,

And, then I knew I would never spend another night alone.

He is a shell, hollowed out from the man I knew before,

But, I have all the missing pieces, I saved them to restore,

There will be a period of adjustment, to be true,

But we will work it out, between me and you.

You have done great things, been a hero, this is so true

Compared my quiet sacrifices, who was the hero, me or you

If you have never experienced selfless love, you have missed one of the greatest of human experiences.

First moron: They say life is a cycle.

Second moron: No wonder my legs are always so tired.

With enough humility, meekness, gentleness, people will mistake you for a big person.

Don't automatically assume someone is a slackard just because he never wins first place, He may be working harder for what he gets than someone with much more talent who gets first place.

Talking is not necessarily communicating.

How do you find peace with someone who deliberately and maliciously causes you harm-you forgive them, they have to live with themselves, you don't.

Winners keep winning because they keep finding a way to win, for any resistance or obstacle, they go over it, around it or through it, just never give up, so, even if you're behind don't give up because the race is not over until the final bell.

18

THE GOOD OLD DAYS

We talk and vdream about the good old days where our memory pulls up a simpler time of less stress, friendlier, less regulations, more freedoms, stronger family bonds, while the memory washes over the everyday facts such as no air conditioning, no-indoor plumbing, no refrigerators, no washing machines, houses you froze in the winter time and burned up in the summer time, and there were no antibiotics, and walking was the main source of transportation, work was 10-12 hours a day, 6 days a week-that part doesn't sound so good, but, it was a time when a friend was friend no matter what, a person's word was worth a hundred contracts, where family was treasured, and honor, respect and loyalty were the norms-now that was the good old days.

Money will buy you all the sex you can stand, but not love.

Maude: Don't you think marriage is romantic?

Claude: like standing in an ant bed.

Life is not a spectator sport, get in the game.

It's amazing how many people who never have anything to say, always want to have the last word.

Old procrastinators never die, they keep putting it off.

Being beside yourself does not mean you have a twin.

Life without honor is no life at all.

Quitting should be our last option.

Givers should only give to givers, make the takers work for it.

Claude: If I went far away, would you try to get me back?

Maude: How far?

We could all see the forest if we could just get those damned trees out of the way.

Old religious people never die, they just congregate.

Always do things that are great, and when your time comes, God may allow you to be a little late.

There are many ways to get the job done, it doesn't always have to be your way.

Don't give up on love, because sooner or later, love will find a way.

First moron: Do you believe there is a pot of gold at the end of the rainbow?

Second moron: No, if there were, my ex-wife would have found it by now.

Why is almost everything a 64 dollar question?

If it's good enough to say, then it's good enough to do.

Old insomniacs never die, they just wait to yawn at dawn.

Chocolate was invented by the devil.

Sin occupies a dark corner of your heart.

19

THE LAST WORD

My dear friend, my best friend, I know I have hurt you deeply, and how can I ever possibly make amends. To hurt your best friend, takes time, it just doesn't come quickly. With your friends, especially your best friend, you spend some of the best moments of your life. You spend much time with him with both the fun and the grief. And, of course you compete, have arguments, each pushing to outdo the other, teasing and laughing, always trying to get "one up" on the other. Talk, man -o- man did we talk, about all the problems of life, love, responsibility, wisdom, politics, the future, and came up with answers-some actually sounding sane.

Over time we developed a deep understanding of each other, our feelings, our fears, our strengths and our weaknesses. It is that knowledge that can allow us to hurt and harm those that are close to us like we could never do to a stranger, especially our best friend. So why did I do it? Why did I hurt him so badly? I should have stopped, but no, I had to win, had to top him, had to beat him at the word game, outdo him one more time, and nothing was going to hold me back. So when all else failed for me to push over the top to victory, to get in the last word, I struck him with words that cut him deep, words that hit his weakest place, a place only a good friend would know.

I knew instantly that my mouth had moved faster than my brain, my drive to win, to get that last word had clouded my judgment for he fell silent, the silence almost like thunder in my head. His chin fell, his eyes turned slowly away and he stared at the ground, and saw his shoulders drop as if a heavy weight had been place on them. I wanted to speak, to say something to ease the pain I had just caused, but my tongue felt thick and heavy, I could not get it to move, my head was splitting, as I felt the blood drain from my head. I stood still, frozen by the horror I had just done. In a few moments that seemed forever, he quietly turned and walked away. I wanted a baseball bat to beat myself over the head. Then came all the recriminations, the what-ifs-what if I had not done this or had not done that and what if I say this or do that, can I undo my awful deed. It's said that time heals all wounds-not true, some wounds never heal-I just hope and pray this is not one of them. I certainly understand now that having the last word at any cost is costly.

Nascar drivers are the only ones who can do it in a circle at 200 miles per hour for three hours and not get dizzy.

The best way to keep friends is to forgive them when they fail you.

For some reason or other, habits seem to be repetitive.

If you have to make one choice between love, money, or happiness, choose love,

because with it, you will find happiness, and whatever money you have will be enough.

Aspire to greatness, that way anything less is beneath you.

Claude: I should have been a pimp.

Maude: Apparently, you have forgotten how we met.

Mankind is not yet fully domesticated.

20

FROM ME TO WE

There was a time when our brotherhood,

Was a thing that was ever so good,

When helping others was not a chore,

And in your time of need many were at your door.

People would give of their time and ear,

And, we all moved forward without any fear,

To fall down was not such a disgrace,

Someone would always step in and take your place.

While some gave a helping and lifting hand,

Others were guiding and mentoring you to be a man,

Our neighbor was also our friend,

Our friend was right back a neighbor again.

It was just us, it was deep in our soul,

It made every one of us into a great whole,

Then came the dividers taking us back to one,

And much damage to our power of the whole they have done.

They have replaced the we with me,

They say forget we, stand alone and be all you can be,

I think I see why they push for me-ism,

It will cause between us a great schism.

The whole of we and the great things we have done,

Is reduced to only the strength of the power of one,

So we stand alone facing the rigors of life,

And face by our self the cuts and bruises of its strife.

As one, they can bend and break us to their will,

As one, my voice will become silent and still,

But hope never dies even when the voice is still,

Even without a request for my hand, extend it I will.

To everyone, know that I am ready to help, I will say,

Ready to do, ready to go, ready to be there, it's just my way,

Maybe those thoughts will spread to more than just one,

And grow from me to we, and much will be done.

I will not let them take the power of many to do good,

Replace it with the false feeling of power that me would,

I will raise my voice and spread my message true,

That changing me to we will be the best in you.

We will not hesitate, we will not fall,

We will share words of hope, so our goal will not stall,

We each in our own words and in our own way,

Move each other from me to we every day.

Our world had reached a dark place,

Will have beautiful sunlight in its place,

They'll never understand the power of we,

The power of the whole of we, they will never see.

And, on this you can bet my friend,

The power of we to do good will always win.

How many days of man's life will he have to be asked to take out the garbage, all of them

There are many days of rain in a man's life, but after every rain, there is a rainbow.

How to make a marriage fun, make some things predictable, into unpredictable, and some things unpredictable into predictable, but it's going to be rough for a while.

We all can help, just being there is sometimes all that is required.

All you can do is not all you can do when many join in doing all they can do, and what the group can do together is more than the sum total of the individuals.

The sum total of all of it is one person, one couple, one family, one town, one state, one nation, one world.

Always playing it safe will never produce greatness.

If you keep stretching, you will likely reach your goal.

If you look for it and you work hard enough, you can find a beautiful life.

Even the dumbest of us knows the importance of good manners.

Some say that an ounce of prevention is worth a pound of cure, so, if we had a pound of prevention, we might never get sick.

Never fault the falter until you know if the fault was greater than the falter could fathom.

Memories are the closest we get to the real thing.

Give your sub-conscious mind the idle time it needs, it can make connections you can't.

Not everything old is necessarily good, and neither is everything new necessarily bad.

You can be a great person, even if you are the only one who knows it.

21

THE LITTLE MAN

It's the little man who plows the ground to make our food,

It's the little man that paves our roads and builds the bridges,

It's the little man that builds the houses and buildings,

It's the little man that builds the cars, trains and airplanes,

It's the little man who fights the wars, and defends our freedoms,

It's the little man who works and makes our economy strong,

It's the little man who builds the churches and attends services,

It's the little man who forms the fabric and soul of our nation,

Could we pause for a moment and say thanks to the little man.

Find some good in everything you see, add a little good in everything you do, find something positive in everything you hear, and say something worthwhile in everything you say, and most of the time, be a person worthy of our time.

Making the right plug will help with your connections.

Good pride is good for everybody, bad pride, to be good, has to hurt somebody.

Hate in the life of others is easiest seen through the prism of our own.

First moron: Why do so many little boys mis-behave so badly?

Second moron: They're practicing to be adults.

You probably start an endless chain reaction every time you do an act of kindness.

Being jealous is an admission of a particular weakness.

Maude: I'm tired of you lying that you love me.

Claude: So, you really want the truth?

Never say never because you never know when never might happen.

Old broom makers never die, they just get swept away.

There is no greater love than a man lay down his life for a friend, or, is it lay down his wife for a friend, or, is it lay down his friend's wife, but, it's got to be one of them.

Cashier's do it in their drawers.

Love is for sale—think how many products are sold in the name of or the spirit of love in one form or another.

Age old good policies are not just for the old.

Claude: I'm just itching to get my hands on some money.

Maude: I've got some bad news for you, money won't stop the itching.

Old mop makers never die, because that's just the way the mop flops.

Many people lose their way, because they can't find their internal compass.

22

SOMETIMES

Sometimes, it seems everything goes wrong,

Sometimes, we have the worst luck,

Sometimes, we just can't seem to get ahead,

Sometimes, our plans just don't seem to work out,

Sometimes, we just can't seem to get to a happy place,

Sometimes, our friends don't seem to give us support,

Sometimes, the bad seems to outweigh the good,

Sometimes, it seems there is more rain that sun,

Sometimes, it seems we just can't find reason for hope,

BUT THEN,

Sometimes, things go right even when we don't expect it,

Sometimes, we have a run of good luck, and we don't deserve it,

Sometimes, things look up, even when we can't explain it,

Sometimes, things just come together and we have no reason,

Sometimes, we find ourselves feeling happy right where we are,

Sometimes, our friends surprise us with selfless acts of kindness,

Sometimes, the good comes through and outweighs the bad,

Sometimes, there are many sunny days and few with rain,

Sometimes, we find there is much reason to hope,

Sometimes, we find life is really worth living.

AND, SOMETIMES, THAT'S JUST THE WAY IT IS.

Put all your heart in it, and you may get results your eyes can see.

If you look for evil you will most certainly find it.

Maude: My mother said you were not good marriage material.

Claude: You should have listened to your mother.

The riddle of life is explained by purposeful living.

Your dreams are weirdly unique to you.

Sometimes keeping your mouth shut is more than your pride can bear.

The only training for life is on-the-job.

Old wine makers never die, they just age well.

People will get your point, if delivered sharply.

23

THE COMPETITION

After all is said and done,

There's nothing new under the sun,

It started as a friendly kind of competition,

But developed into a self-imposed imposition.

There's this contention between me and you,

And, certainly something that is not new,

As all contenders, we try to bring each other down,

We wait in our corners ready for the next round.

We wait, we watch and we pray,

To see who will survive one more day,

This didn't just start, but way back when,

Even before we saw each other as a friend.

And now, I will tell this tale of woe,

And of the lasting impact on the unlucky trio

And if I never see you again, I will weep,

If I never hear your voice again, hardly will I sleep.

If I never again hold your hand,

I will be an unhappy man,

If I never share again with your time,

There will be loneliness in mine.

Together, we were quite a pair,

Even as we aged and lost our hair,

Yesterday has merged into tomorrow's scene,

And, we got lost in the space in-between.

Yesterday we watched our time go by,

For tomorrow we will hope and sigh,

For we may not be here or remember your name,

Or, even of a time I don't think of you the same.

We both moved merrily down the way,

But, we came to an impossible fork today,

Now, there' a choice to make to our sorrow,

To live in yesterday or move into tomorrow.

She loved us both always and true,

But, unable to choose between me and you,

And, now that we have reached this point in time,

She will be yours, or she will be mine.

It will be hard, but today, she must choose,

One of us will win, the other will lose,

For today, the day that was squeezed in,

Yesterday's regrets gone and tomorrow's begin.

So this is it, right now, today,

But, another place and time, another way,

We will all do the best we can,

Stand tall and be a man.

We do in her decision trust,

In the choosing one of us,

She closed her eyes and said I have to think,

And, her eyes they did not blink.

She opened her eyes and was about to cry,

And our eyes, they were not dry,

I have made my decision today,

And, I will tell you in this way.

I love you both, as you know so well,

More than that, I cannot tell,

The choice was just too hard to do,

Choosing between the two of you.

And when I give you my decision today,

I hope you both will love me anyway,

To choose between you I could not stand,

And, for that I reason I have chosen another man.

Just because you get punished for doing wrong does not mean you will be rewarded for doing right.

Many people spend so much time trying to leave a legacy, they don't have time to live a life worthy of one.

The bad thing about being lonely is you have to do it by yourself.

Just because you can't do everything is not an excuse to do nothing.

24

SOMEBODY

Everyone needs somebody,

Everybody needs someone,

Everyone can be someone,

Everybody can be somebody,

Somebody can be anybody,

Anybody can be everyone,

Someone can be everyone,

Everyone can be somebody.

Your mind can see things that your eyes can't.

Each of us has a load in life to carry, and if a person has no load to carry, then they have no life.

Those who ask you to do bad things probably are only looking for some unsuspecting, gullible person to take the blame while they take the loot.

A balanced life is always teetering.

I'm in the middle part of the lower section of upper part of the bottom of the income chart.

Your mind can see the quality of your soul, and your heart can feel the goodness of your character.

A hug is a band-aid for the soul.

Maude: You're gonna miss me when I'm gone.

Claude: There is always hope.

The way having a piece of sex makes me feel, I don't think I can handle the whole thing.

If there is ever a choice in your life take it, if there is a dark cloud hanging over you, go inside.

Never ask others to do for you what you won't do for yourself.

My mind can reach many things I can't see.

Cooks do it in their apron.

Don't despair if it seems on a particular day everything is going wrong, remember, even the most successful people have such days, and tomorrow will be a new day and can and will most likely be better.

If things don't add up, first check your math.

Random means sooner or later it's you.

Most of our life is spent in just holding on, and waiting for help.

To survive, we need to be like a strip tease artist—just grin and bear it.

25

DON'T AND WON'T

Don't tell me what to do,

I won't tell you what to say,

If we hold these things fast,

We'll have a friendship at last.

You may not always be the best you can be, but you can certainly always can be the best that you are.

First moron: Is kissing contagious?

Second moron: It must be, it is transmitted by mouth.

If you don't believe that all governments are oppressive, try making the income tax voluntary.

The weight of loads we carry in life is reversely proportional to the importance of the load to us.

Share your good fortunes, never your burdens.

We all can help sometimes by just being there and sometimes that is all that is required.

Claude: My mother said you made your living by lifting your skirt.

Maude: Your mother made her living by never putting one on.

One of the good things about sex, is it produces something, but sometimes that's regrettable.

26

POCAHONTAS
THE POEM

You were a stranger when

You came to this land of mine,

The first one I ever saw,

Of people of your kind.

Two people so different,

Yet two spirits of a kind,

Two spirited people,

Same adventurous mind.

We became good friends,

Two of the very best,

My country, me the host,

You the friend, and my guest.

I remembered stories, as the friendship grew,

Of long ago, from my people I knew,

Of the greatest love of all time,

And, a love that comes only to a few.

I see in your eyes,

As you lay by my side,

There is nothing between us,

There is no divide.

You made for me a dream,

where there was none,

Which will stay with me,

When you sail into the sun.

Out by the big blue sea,

we lay under the sun,

Two hearts melted together,

Two hearts became one.

He told me of many things,

Many I never knew,

Of a for-a-way island,

Where green grass grew.

Where men were strong,

And women were fair,

Men who had beards

And women with golden hair

Loving him became easy,

Easy as loving life,

Oh, how I wanted,

To be his wife.

But our ways are so strange,

Our cultures so far apart,

I knew I could only be

His wife in my heart.

Our people are different,

Yet much the same,

Love is always love,

By any other name

You will go far away,

And, I will be sad,

For a few heavenly moments,

I will be forever glad.

Across the big blue water,

My heart will go,

To a far-a-way land,

That I will never know.

When he said farewell,

I knew I would cry,

But, what I really wanted,

Was to lay down and die

I want to build a boat,

As I look out to sea,

And, then go sailing

Where the winds are calling me.

I'll sail to lands unknown,

And search out every place,

Until I find this man,

And once again, touch his face.

Love is never lost,

When once it is found,

Love goes and grows

On memory's fertile ground.

In all my memories,

I became his wife,

Forever, I'll hold those memories,

And memories will be my life.

People can be generous by giving to those in need because they are giving from what they have earned. Governments cannot give because they don't earn, they can only redistribute from what they take.

Being a minority of one viewpoint does not mean you are probably wrong, what it does mean is you are probably not right.

Humans are very complex, and if they weren't, there would be no lawyers.

Good answers don't come easy.

The easiest way to have a wonderful life is to have a life that's full of wonder.

Old grievers never die, they just wait for the mourning.

Your last chance doesn't always come at the end.

Dare yourself to be brave.

Boxers do it in their shorts.

In some cases, love is a swell event.

Had you rather be on the low scale of being right or the high scale of being wrong?

Dumb: They say tomorrow never comes.

Dumber: Oh, it will definitely come if you have a bad hangover.

You can't find the answer if you haven't figured out the question.

Everyone is always looking for the smoking gun—I didn't know guns had any tobacco.

First moron: I was asking my girl to marry me, and was arrested.

Second moron: For what, begging without a license?

On one side of the scales you have pride, greed, lust, envy, gluttony, wrath and sloth, and on the other side you have love, and love wins most the time.

Choose your battles carefully, because in many there can be no winner.

27

PEACE

First I wonder,

Then I dream,

Then I think,

Then I believe,

Then I want,

Then I do,

Then I get,

Then I share,

Then I have peace.

Humility is a necessary ingredient to true power.

See the world through one eye with caution and suspicion, and with the other, look out and see the world through the eye of a child.

Why would anybody with half a brain ever partner up with a crook, a liar or a thief, you would be volunteering to be his next victim.

Love much, hate little, laugh a lot, laugh at yourself often, wish happiness to everyone including yourself, give of yourself much, ask for forgiveness often, and give it to everyone whether they ask for it or not, and give thanks regularly, then my friend, you will live a happy balanced life.

Dumb: What does a king, a sentence and gossip have in common?

Dumber: A subject.

The very best you can be is not always required.

Don't just stand there – do something – worthwhile.

Why is it that a person with a thick head has thin thoughts?

Old dentist never die, they just get crowned.

Not every rattle leads to a snake.

There seems to be a shortage of love, perhaps we should all get together and make some.

If someone gives you their heart, handle it will care, for if you don't, that proves you probably didn't have one, and they may come take theirs back, and you definitely will be without one.

Good pretending is not a pretense.

A feeding frenzy does not mean anyone gets to eat.

Claude: I think I have been living in hell.

Maude: Keep talking like that and you may get a first-hand look.

The solution for worry is work.

Don't let your life be over before you start living it.

If you blame someone else for all your sins they can't be forgiven.

If you don't know whether or not you know, then either will serve you equally well, so just pick one.

The way some Christians behave, you would think they don't believe in God.

You had better watch carefully, it's hard to see tragedy coming.

Some say only the strong will survive, but probably it's only the strong willed will survive.

If I had everything I have ever wanted, I would have an ocean full of crap.

First moron: Hey, I just noticed your watch is stopped.

Second moron: Yeah, I would take it in for repair, but, I just don't have the time.

We don't always let our best feelings show, and off on many a trip of self-interest we go.

Making believe prepares you for the real thing.

A sure fire thing does not require flame.

There's never been a better time to do the right thing than right now.

No freedom comes without sacrifice.

Greed for power has a new weapon-greed is not for the taker, but for someone else in need, so therefore you can't object, the word that describes that is socialism.

Maude: I'm unhappy, just take me back where you found me.

Claude: You're probably too old to walk the streets now.

You can love the outdoors, love the land, the water, nature, books, music, but with that and no person to love, life is barely worth living.

Anger seeks its own level against others, and we are the fool when we allow such foolishness.

Everybody can be good at something, even if it's only sitting quietly and not complaining.

There is never a right time to do the wrong thing, and never a wrong time to do the right thing.

Adultery has now reached a sad state of affairs.

If you want people to notice you more, the next time they ask for volunteers, raise your hand.

Old Olympic runners never die, they just pass the torch.

Sex carries with it responsibilities, so don't screw around with it.

Old people who draw water from a well never die, they just kick the bucket.

It is never too late for an early start.

Never make a threat that you can't 100% backup, otherwise you will lose all credibility.

Maude: Many men could have chosen me, you're lucky you did.

Claude: Not as lucky as they are.

There are some people who don't deserve help, but we usually help them anyway.

Old jailed prisoners never die, they hang in there.

Nobody remembers second place victories.

28

YOUR WAY

For every season,

There is a reason,

for every person or thing

A purpose it will bring.

Before day is done,

There's a race to be won,

We likely make our quest,

When we do our best.

It's sad to say,

It's not everyone's way,

You can be a star,

By being more than you are.

One person's desire,

Can set the world on fire,

Give hope to those,

Whose spirits have not rose.

You have promises to keep,

No time to sleep,

Be more than what you say,

Start with some good today.

You can pass the test

By doing it with zest,

So, for sure at the end of the day,

You'll have done it your way.

And, lend a helping hand,

To one who is trying to stand,

For those who need, always be near,

And, no one will wonder why you are here.

So, at the end of the day,

You will have done good, your way.

Everybody wants patience, but most just can't wait for it.

Thought is the way the mind can travel.

Pretending can sometimes seem so real, but that may just put a supposition.

Maude: Mother said she was coming and was going to show you a thing or two.

Claude: I'm nauseous just thinking about it.

Old bomb makers never die, they just have a blast.

The opposite of so far so good is so little so bad, check your progress.

I have so much love for myself, there is plenty left over for you.

Do your best at what you do best and you won't need luck,

Luck is needed when you don't do your best at what you do best.

I wish my brain was like a computer, so I could push a button and delete all the junk.

If you stop to wonder, people will wonder why you stop.

Perception is only half of the successful trip, the rest is up to you.

We could explain everything if we just believed in magic.

You pay your money and take your chances presumes you have some of each.

When I go to the motivational meetings where everybody gets fired up, I always carry a bucket of water, just in case.

29

A WAY OUT

_____

I don't have anything like a claim to fame,

Unfortunately, I don't have even a claim,

Others are claiming ownership of these and those,

My offer is my sad tale, and that's how it goes.

Others are pronouncing great things they have done,

I can't think of one single battle that I have ever won,

I don't want a picture of sackcloth and ash,

But sometimes I get the feeling that I am just trash.

And so, after all, I'm alone and out in the cold,

I'm getting to feel forgotten and old,

No one to look or see and take notice of my plight,

No one to cut through the darkness and shed a little light.

Perhaps it's time to yield and kneel down and pray,

For I will not let my spirit break, it's just not my way,

For deep within there's still a spark of might,

I'll nurture it in every way, and grow into light.

Others can't help me, they don't even see me,

And, even if they did, they would just let me be,

But, I see a plan now that's coming to mind,

I'll go to each and every one and spend some time.

I'm sure there are helpful things for each that I can do,

They will never hear about me, but what can I do for you,

Then they may see me not as bother, but as a man,

I'll extend to them kindness, as much as I can.

They will all become a little dependent on me,

I'll be as encouraging and helpful as I can be,

I no longer need them to help me out and up,

By accepting these things from me, they have set me free.

I have found my purpose and so my life will go,

I can achieve peace and happiness, this I know,

By doing, all these things for them, but really for me,

I have become whole, this I now see.

No one will ever hear or know, no one will ever see,

That I'm a hero, even if it's known only by me.

One who has the last word will definitely be remembered if he is the one whose plan didn't work.

They say it is a calculated risk, what isn't?

Many people take forever trying to make a long story short.

Maude: Will you love me when I am old and fat.

Claude: Looks that way.

How can you be expected to make wise, intelligent decisions, when you've never seen one?

I could be wrong, but that doesn't automatically make you right.

Having the punishment fit the crime is no deterrent, the punishment should be 2 or 3 times the crime.

Old lovers never die, they just swoon along.

Maude: You make love like no man I have ever known.

Claude: How many have you known.

Not all old men are wise.

30

SOMEDAY

Someday, the greed won't exceed the need,

Someday, the cruel won't be allowed to rule,

Someday, the sad will almost all be glad,

Someday, the hate will definitely abate,

Someday, those left behind will always be on our mind,

Someday, those lying in the sand will be given a helping hand,

Someday, those who are hungry will live without that misery,

Someday, war will be no more,

Someday, there will be love like that from above,

Someday, the game won't be shame,

Someday, all men, each individually, will be a friend,

Someday, we'll each reach a place of grace,

Someday, our might all together will make right,

Someday, we'll live the best way every day,

Someday, there'll be a time when no one is left behind,

Someday, we can live because we forgive,

Someday, there'll be a way for each one to have his say,

Someday, the only thing left is just our self,

Someday, we will make more than we take,

Someday, we will give so we can live,

Someday, we will all stand tall,

Someday, you can bet we'll have no regret,

Someday, there will be a rain that will wash away all our pain,

Someday, we'll run and not be outdone,

Someday, there will be more to us than just lust,

Someday, our main feature will be a noble creature,

Someday, those with a lot will share with those who have not,

Someday, after all the rest, we will be at our best,

Someday, many will share the burdens others bear,

Someday, people will think and of knowledge drink,

Someday, the needy at your door will need no more,

Someday, a chain of good deeds will begin and it will never end,

Someday, everything good will be where it should,

Someday, the tide will turn and humans will finally learn,

Someday, in some distant year, lessons of the past will be clear,

Someday, there will be no sorrow, but it won't be tomorrow,

Someday, hostilities will cease, and there will be peace,

Someday, every me will grow into we,

Someday, all the loose talk will take a walk,

Someday, after where you have been, you will still have a friend,

Someday, what you don't know won't be so,

Someday, people will be good, as they should,

Someday, doing right will shine some light,

Someday, your friends around will keep you from going down,

Someday, you'll listen one day and know what to say,

Someday, you'll find a safe place, but pray, just in case,

Someday, beyond here is an answer or two, the rest is up to you.

Someday, may it come soon.

Always assume your opponent is better than you think he is.

In the springtime, a young man's fancy turns to love, and in the summer and in the fall, and doubly in the winter.

Being young and immature doesn't fully explain it, but adding stupid does.

Old baseball players never die, they just steal home.

There's nothing more infuriating than a braggart who has in fact done everything he says.

Not every good deed is good.

We each have our own demons to deal with that no one else knows about.

Don't be a copycat, be the cat that the copycat's want to copy.

Someday is the day when we expect something great, grand, glorious or unique, but today is the day we plan for someday.

It doesn't cost anymore, so dream big.

Don't harden your heart because of the wrongs of a few, but open your heart to the good of many.

If you see both what comes around and what goes around means you are in the middle.

The ladder of success always has at least one more step beyond where you are.

31

PATH TO YOUR CAREER

If you are having trouble choosing a path to take for your career, take each option one at a time, and for several days, every time you have some idle time, visualize yourself in the career, and in your mind, go through the motions, the work you would do, the interaction with others that is required, the resistance to you and your ideas and plans, and how to counter them. In other words, live out in your mind a fairly lengthy sampling of that career and see how it feels and if it seems to fit, do that for each option that you are seriously considering, and there is a good chance you will be able to correctly pick one

---

You can lead a horse to water, but you can't make him drink, just be happy you got him there.

I don't want to dream of rags to riches I want to dream of riches to more riches.

If you don't like the rules, then find another game.

There is a point at which acts of kindness become offensive.

Sometimes getting a piece of the action can have a bad reaction.

Maude: You're going to hell.

Claude: I'll hold the gate open for you.

Just because you ask the question does not necessarily mean you know the answer.

It's not that I don't have much of a vocabulary, I just don't have much to say.

Everybody hates a bully, even bullies.

Always plan for something bigger than what you are.

Do something Divine, forgive someone when you don't want to and who does not deserve it.

It is always easier to complain than to work.

If you can't say it, then you don't know it.

Be careful what you ask for, things going away from you look totally different than those things coming at you.

If it seems your friends don't like you so much, find some that don't know you so well.

It does not prove you care by forcing someone else to share.

Absent minded people can't remember where they do it.

Old pilots never die, they just get high.

I would give you all my love but that would leave me with none

Putting your best foot forward is difficult if you don't know.

First moron: They say teach a child and he will not depart from it.

Second moron: I guess that's why so many adults act like children.

We are constant being told to stand by, don't let it apply to your life.

You'll never be a leader if you always wait for somebody to tell you what to do.

Just hold on a little while longer, chaos like everything else, doesn't last forever.

32

PAINTING MY OLD TRUCK

It will take more than a little luck,

For me to paint my old truck

It did nothing but just sat there,

And, was obviously totally unaware.

Of all the sweat and cussing,

That would come to bear.

I just stood and stared at it in vain,

Hoping to put it off with a little rain.

But, if I was going to get this done,

I was going to need a little sun.

The thought of sanding all that rust so red,

Made me want to go back to bed.

But, if I am really going to do it,

I needed to stand up like a man and get to it.

My Wife says it is an awful sight,

I think it would look good at a dogfight.

Besides I may need it in the long haul,

Like when my drinking buddies call.

She said get rid of all the rust she saw,

Or, she'd get a higher power, my mother-in-law.

And, every job should be thought through,

So, I went back in inside got a cold brew.

I sat down and started to think,

About that rust, but mostly about my drink.

I seriously needed to make a plan,

Or, come up with an excuse that would stand.

But, after I had downed a cold pack of six,

My mind began playing dirty little tricks.

And, though I need to get started on that plan,

The hard cold fact is I can hardly stand.

Maybe the painting job needs a real pro,

Not some backwoods redneck so and so.

The thought of all that rust blowing in the breeze,

Just thinking of it, makes me want to sneeze.

It would certainly be bad for the nose,

And, would ruin my only good work clothes.

And, all the problems ahead I see,

Makes me think this job may not be for me.

But, Unless I do it, there will be a price to pay,

And, definitely no rolling in the hay.

I also believe this thought to be right,

There won't be any more afternoon delight.

She will be in from her trip soon,

And, its already four hours past noon,

I may get out of this under this guise,

I'll sneak out with a homemade disguise,

Out into wide underground I'll go,

For I may residing there for a millennium or so.

It's time to move, to go full throttle,

So, I grabbed another long neck bottle.

I want to say woe is me, but what the hell,

All days are pretty much alike, best I can tell.

Some days are really cold, and some are hot,

All the others I seem to have forgot.

So, I'll stand my ground and no other,

If that doesn't work, I'll go home to mother.

I have thought hard on how to get this job done,

But I see on the horizon, a setting sun,

Surely, it's too late to start today,

Wasn't I supposed to do it next Saturday, anyway?

All this thinking has been tough,

I'll bet tonight is really gonna be rough.

But here's what I'm gonna do,

And, I'm gonna pass it along to you,

But, I'll tell you with this little note,

Monday I'm going to the body shop and get a quote.

There are many things in life that you know are right or wrong without having experienced them.

The first one to fall is just as much a hero as the last one to stand.

To protect yourself, be open and receptive to all ideas, but also suspicious and distrusting of them.

We are all here for a reason, the challenge is for each of us to figure out what.

People are not necessarily more likely to do good or bad, but they are certainly more likely to do what they believe is in their own best interest.

If you have nowhere to go, then that's where you will go.

The survival of mankind came as a result of the unbelievable adaptability of the human race to adversity.

Never bet your bread money, or you may be left with neither.

Sometimes the least of these can be the best of those.

Dumb: They say to use your time wisely.

Dumber: I would, but I don't have any left.

The cost of your time is priceless.

Everybody wants something.

33

FROM HEAVEN

It always has been and is still a mystery,

About this thing of me and you,

Our love so wonderful and so fine,

And such love is known only to a lucky few.

Everything about us has worked very well,

It was so obvious that everyone could tell,

We had the best any couple could make.

In everything we did show understanding and care,

And much patience, kindness and love we did share,

Where and when and how it all came to be.

No one has the words to describe, not even me.

I don't accept magic, it's just not in my book,

But then, maybe I should take another look.

I know not from whence and where it came,

But, the beauty of it tells me that there is no other the same.

Maybe I shouldn't think, or worry about it or fret,

Just accept and live and enjoy the best I can get,

But, it does raise and stir up a conundrum or two,

And, if I did anything at all, what did I do?

So, I will just live and live in the mystery and smile,

And, enjoy the tender feelings all the whole while,

There was something that caused this wonderful event,

And whatever it was, it must have been heaven sent.

I could tell you more, but I am waiting to see if you have learned anything so far.

Never having a reason before is reason enough.

Human character is built like a stair case, one step at a time.

Claude: When I die, will I be remembered?

Maude: For what?

Old mediators never die, they just reach a compromise.

Remember the lessons of the past, prepare for the challenges of the future, but live, really live today.

My definition of love is to give, so may you give much.

A stingy tip is an insult, so either gives a generous tip or none at all.

When you finally run out of questions, try coming up with some answers

Old fortune tellers never die, they just can't see it in their future.

Don't say there is nothing you can do, you can always be quiet.

I know it's hard for you to hear, with all that noise coming out of your mouth.

Try to listen, someone may say something worth hearing.

Between a man and a woman, sex can be a hard issue.

Some day we will discard all the emotional trash and finally stand up straight and tall.

Always be kind, because you never know who's keeping notes.

Most of the time, the person standing in your way is you.

We all live under the same sky, clear and bright or dark and cloudy, so don't blame the weather for your failures.

There is a reason behind every reason.

Never ask someone to do for you something that you won't do for yourself.

Never waste good advice on a fool.

Don't pray for the result, pray for the courage to make the result.

Maude: You'll never have another like me.

Claude: Thank you Lord.

As I get older, I know I am wiser, but there is so much to know, so much I should know. I do know I won't ever know all there is to know or even a significant part of it, but maybe I'll learn enough of the parts that I need to know to survive.

We have a limited number of minutes, so make every one of them count.

Old adulterers never die, they just live forever in fear of getting caught.

They say there is safety in numbers, but not if there is not a common cause.

Someday, believe it or not, there will be peace.

I have stayed in up late many a night wondering why the wicked get no rest.

If I had a nickel, I would owe a dime.

Greed has no end, but then, neither does love.

Old seamstresses never die, they just get hemmed in.

A person who hates someone who hates is also a hater.

Learn from your mistakes before you forget them, or likely you will repeat them.

There are many ways to do things wrong, but only a few ways to do them right.

Laughter is the oil between the gears of your mind.

Tears are the safety valve of your heart.

There is no medicine for stupidity.

When fire goes out, the embers still glow, when the love dies out, the feeling will still show.

When I was young, I thought love was the greatest thing, now that I'm older, I think it might be cheese doodles.

If you want to have a better trip next time, remember how you got where you are this time.

I am always straining to hear what I want, but can't shut off what I don't.

If you marry a woman who has been around the block a few times at least you won't get lost.

I asked my girl to marry me and she said no, and I said, I guess I'll have to take that three carat diamond ring back-we're getting married this Saturday.

If you stand up for the right thing, you may get to stay seated for many others-but, there are no guarantees.

Claude: You are always against what I say.

Maude: It is not your words I am against.

If you are going to be a leader, be a good one, and if you are going to be a follower, be a good one, for both are required for a successful society.

Is the world getting better? two-two steps forward, one step backward, is still progress.

How to keep a woman happy – every day tell her you love her, and every day, tell her you're sorry, doesn't matter for what – if you haven't done something to be sorry for by the time you tell her you love her, you probably will before the day is done.

If you have to explain why you are late, don't have to do it without being prepared.

When I was young, I was taught that wisdom would come if I did certain things, now that I am older, I can't remember what those things are.

Choosing things that are neither too high or too low, too much or too little, too deep or too shallow, too good or too bad, too wide or too thin, too rich or too poor, too big or too small, leaves you right where you are.

If you really want to be my friend and help me, then help me with what I need, not what I want.

Old carpet layers never die, they just get laid, or just cut a rug.

It goes like this, start on time, finish late, start late, finish later, start early, finish even later. I give up.

Love does not conquer all, but makes you irrational enough to believe it does.

You will not become more, simply because I become less.

Never give away what you can sell.

They say get a lease on life, I think we know who the landlord is.

It's a good thing when the person inside is as big as the person is outside.

Never do for somebody what they can do for themselves.

Children can be the most frustrating joy in the world.

Can't never could, and, will never will.

When the greed for money or power exceeds moral courage, the road to tyranny has begun.

34

TO MY WIFE, MARIA

I had a dream just the other day,

That life was good, more than I could say.

Even the skies were a bright blue,

And, I was happy just being with you.

Then I awoke and found it was no dream,

Even though real, that's the way it did seem,

You are the reason it's not a dream, but true,

The rudder guiding my life is you.

You just whisper softly in my ear,

And gone is my every fear,

Your smile, that intriguing look,

I have pictured it in my mind's book.

Your touch, your kind eyes,

Assures me of no goodbyes.

All your warmth and charm,

I want to hold forever in my arms.

Holding you close to me so tight,

Makes everything seem all right.

Also, holding you this way,

Makes a sad world go away.

Just being you, the way you are,

Makes my future bright as a star,

Our being together, so right and true,

Because of the goodness of you.

I see the fullness of our love,

Raining down on us from above,

No doubt your hand in mine,

Was meant to be for all time.

When I need you, you're always there,

With you, no burden is to big to bear,

And, when it's you I am thinking of,

There's no problem too big to solve.

They're wrong that love doesn't shine,

You light my path all the time.

And with that light I see,

The greatness that everyone can be.

The grace and patience in your speech,

Inspires belief that everything is within reach.

For all these things you made me more,

Than all I could have ever hoped for.

I love you, and I love my life,

For God in his kindness,

Has loaned me an angel for my wife.

Perhaps the loudest sounds we will ever hear are the whispered words I love you.

Even if you had all the answers, what would you do with them?

Sometimes good things just happen, and sometimes bad things happen, not because we deserve either, but the way we respond to each will determine our future.

I've never been one for pomp and circumstance, I paid my money and I will take my chance.

Claude: If you dislike me so much, why did you marry me?

Maude: Everybody has their moment of weakness, besides, you were my only offer.

People don't want you to carry them, they just want you to walk with them, and every once in a while shut up and listen.

Patience is not putting off until tomorrow what you should do today—the correct word is lazy.

You don't always have to win, sometimes just surviving is good enough.

You can lose your temper, give out expletives, but never, ever lose your perspective.

I don't know about you, but on those governmental forms where you identify your sex with an M or an F, I just don't think much or frequently applies to many people.

I don't trust anybody but me, and I am beginning to have some serious reservations about me.

Old actors never die, they just pretend to.

Someday forgiveness will be more important than pride.

They say always watch out for the unknown-I'm still thinking on that one.

Sometimes you can see with your heart what your eyes can't.

The easy chair prepares you for nothing but a bad back.

If you don't expect much out of people that's what you usually get.

If you raise a lot of sand you're gonna get dirty.

Looking for a lasting moment may take awhile.

Being ever so near but ever so far is ever so true.

35

FINDING THE TOWN

Why is it when you are going uptown, it's the same place as when you go downtown, and you can go out of town, when you've never been in town, and you can be around town, but be in town or out of town, and being out of town doesn't mean you have left town, and the heart of town may not be anywhere near the center, and the fringe of the town may be next to the center, and the center may be uptown, or downtown, and you can be at any of these places and never move. Awesome.

Just being yourself might leave you with no friends.

Someday hope will prevail over despair.

There are a few things more pleasant than to see a happy baby who is smiling.

If the road to success were easy, there would be massive traffic jams.

You have to get your hands dirty before you can get down to the nitty gritty.

Everybody has their moment of weakness, mine is a minute, or an hour, a day or a month.

Doing it the hard way is the only way.

There is only one thing better than a good thing—two.

A soft life leads to a soft belly.

The best way not to show your ass is to close your mouth.

Old mid-wives never die, they just wait to be delivered.

The lower I go, the more people I see, I know.

Being rich in spirit is not affected by the stock market.

The measure of a full life is to have done more good things that you can't remember, than bad ones you can.

The balance of nature requires a perpetual inequality.

Dumb: You told me your brother thinks he is a rooster, what did you do?

Dumber: Nothing, our alarm clock is broken.

The socialist pushes for his brand of equality until we're sore, so that when he gets it, he will have even more.

Dumb: I'm getting where I can't tell right from wrong.

Dumber: You are in luck, the Sheriff can.

If this life is the first chapter, then I am eager to see the second.

The objection to marriage is you have to have a spouse.

A well thought out decision can still be irrational.

There is a great difference between the last man standing, and the last man kneeling.

Old pessimist never die, they just believe they are in the half full of it.

Old ice makers never die, they just chill out.

36

ONE MORE

One more row to hoe,

One more truth to know,

One more hill to climb,

One more victory will be mine,

One more person to befriend,

One more friendly story to spin,

One more sad story to hear and then,

One more heart that's mine to win.

Dare to be different, forgive your enemies, everybody forgives their friends.

Be thankful today, tomorrow you may not get the chance.

Stop waiting for manna to fall out from the sky, go out and plough the corn.

Remember, no matter how hard you work, how much you believe, some things were just never meant to be.

Just because you gain a new friend does not mean you have to lose one.

Maude: Do you remember the words honor and provide for?

Claude: Better than you remember cling only to him.

Old sword swallowers never die, they just get choked up.

Love seems to go to those who already have some.

If you have fear of something, then you have two enemies.

You do not have to agree to be agreeable.

Patience waits for no one.

Love is a little like magic, when you lose it, it can re-appear almost anywhere, anytime.

Never answer a question to which you have given no thought.

Even a fool is smart enough to not fool around.

The smarter you are, the more you understand how little you know.

Doctors need a nurse to help them do it.

The difference between can and cannot is not not.

It's easy to love everybody, but hard to help just one.

Your brain will tell you how much to give, but it will never be 100% without emotion.

All animals kill for food or protection, but only humans kill for many other reasons.

Old farmers never die, they become grim reapers.

Old mid-wives never die, they are waiting to be delivered.

37

OUR DESTINY

We, together, will all persevere,

Because our greatness is near,

We shall each grasp and hold fast,

So peace will come at last.

We help each one stand,

So each can become his own man,

We can give so very much,

So we can share the human touch.

Those who harm, we will forgive,

So we both can have honor and live,

Friends and alliances it will take,

For the good we intend to make.

None of us may look the same,

But, from a common source we came,

Every human has a brain and heart,

We can feel, we can be smart.

And, we want for everyone we know,

A chance to live, learn and grow,

When we want each other to survive,

Then human race will live and thrive.

For, I promise to do my part, you see,

My hope is you will do the same for me,

When the dust of eternity settles and is still,

Our destiny will have reached God's will.

The person who thinks he understands everything doesn't realize how much there is to know.

If you want to fight, there is always someone else just like you.

People with split personalities should never be lonely.

People who find what they want, change their mind very quickly when they find it.

Complaining just makes it worst, even the bottom is on top of something.

The higher you go, there is less competition, but better.

Good answers usually don't come easy.

Maude: What are you doing to do when I leave?

Claude: Give thanks.

If you think you are absolutely certain that you are right, then think again.

Only the human race could evolve with a genetic code where $1 + 1 = 3$.

The surprise element does not work for me, everybody always sees me coming.

Don't let your hang-ups get you locked up.

The truth changes everything.

Listening to a man of few words can be a pleasure, but to a man of many words can be torture.

They say a cat has nine lives, you unfortunately, only have one, so you had better make it count.

If you are lucky enough to have good health, you need to thank somebody for it.

It is unfortunate that the person who has a flat tire on the way to work will exclaim-I have the worst luck, everything happens to me, while he forgets to mention that it has been 12 years, 2 months, 14 days and 6 hours that he has traveled to work and did not have a flat tire

Claude: Marriage is the toughest thing I have ever known.

Maude: Just wait 'til I divorce you.

They say there is only one alternative, but if there is only one, there is no alternative.

Old clock makers never die, they just wind down.

I'm not detached from reality, I'm just exploring the improbable.

38

NO DOUBT

Let there be no doubt,

what this story is about,

it's about raunchy men,

sexy women and sin.

As sure as Heaven, as sure as Hell,

Man's wickedness is why he fell

The brain searches out the best fit answer, the mind determines if it is rational, and the heart determines if it's is evil or good.

True, a rising tide floats all boats, but a tide that rises too quickly, sinks all boats.

True greatness is not based on how many people you can help on your way up, it's how many you can help on your way down.

The way to totalitarianism and loss of freedom is by doing it in small increments, and convincing people each little increment is good for them.

Sometimes that little inner voice has great words of wisdom—so why aren't you listening.

Don't tell me where to go if you've never been there.

Why is it that we can't forget what we should and we remember everything we shouldn't.

Never underestimate the power of power.

Never wait for tomorrow to put off something that you can go ahead and put off today.

Old arsonists never die, they just flame out.

How to forget something you should but can't-pretend it's your car keys.

If you set your sights too high, you will stumble over things.

Dumb: Do you think humans are getting smarter?

Dumber: We fight wars we can't win, spend money we don't have, give up our freedom for non-existent security, and, idiots with no brains do all the talking, so, the answer is obviously no.

A person will stay down only by choice.

I see why you don't believe in yourself, take a look at yourself and you will see why too.

Life is not a spectator sport.

It looks like the only way we can have peace is to go to war.

You can never get back what you didn't put in.

The naked truth about sex is its better naked.

You don't have to carry the whole world on your back if you have it in your hand.

If you don't know where you are going, stay put, and at least you will learn a little about your surroundings.

39

PERFECTLY CLEAR

Let's make this perfectly clear, the things you do after the things you do before the things you do after the things you do before the things you do after, will be greatly influenced by the things you do before the things you do after the things you do before.

Here is some good news, you can be better than you are.

Never regret your regrets, it proves your conscience is still working.

All the good people I've never met, is one of my greatest regrets

When my conscience reddens my face, probably means I'm in the wrong place.

Maude: What do you think about life after marriage?

Claude: What life?

Always use clean words, because you never know when you might have to eat them.

Life is not easy, and if you don't believe me, try living it.

Humor is so important, it's no longer a laughing matter.

If a bell rang every time God gave us a blessing, we would all be deaf.

Every time you reach for a higher goal, may you always find a handle. H is for Hell, and if we could take Hell out of whine, we could all be feeling good very soon.

I'll be all right if I can just make it to the weekend, and every week has a weekend.

Every Grappling with life is like holding a tiger by the tail, it's hard to hold on, but you can't let go.

Every time you give a piece of your heart, it grows back bigger than before.

Ridiculing someone beneath you places you below them.

It's been said that God is watching from a distance, I hope his eyesight is not too good.

Claude: You ask me to make love to you all night, what kind of man do you think I am?

Maude: I don't know, but we are about to find out.

If you want love, then go find it, it will not hunt you down and drag you away.

Wishing and hoping sometimes gets mistaken for resolve and hard work.

Maude: You sure do have a lot of hair on your chest.

Claude: Better me than you

Coming clean usually means more than a bath.

Lazy people don't do it.

Sometimes in life, the hardest thing to hold is our tongue.

Dumb: You are only worth the value of your words

Dumber: No wonder I'm so broke.

40

REASON TOGETHER

Come let us reason together

To reason, we must be rational,

To be rational, we must have understanding

To be understanding, we must be receptive,

To be receptive, we must be accommodating,

To be accommodating, we must be generous,

To be generous, we must be caring,

To be caring, we must have feelings,

To have feelings, we must have love,

To have love, we must build the right attitude,

To have the right attitude, you must love yourself.

To love yourself, actions must equal conscience,

And if so, then let us come reason together.

These days, no one takes advice, not even their own.

Don't let your alligator mouth over rule your tadpole brain.

I conquered all my fears by replacing them with phobias.

I keep having dizzy spells, but then, the earth keeps turning around and around.

They say humans are getting smarter, but then I look at the latest generation and I have serious doubts.

No matter the status of your life, be thankful for it, you could lose it.

Maude: You don't give me the time of day.

Claude: So, get a watch.

I am not hesitating, I am just giving the world one more chance.

A leader is something you train yourself to be.

Newsflash, you don't have to be a genius to do things smartly.

Remember 3 things, be good, be careful, and be thankful.

In almost all cases, whatever is holding you back, you can overcome.

Old friends never die, they live on in our hearts and memories.

Which is more important, success or happiness?-yes, I'm asking

Some say life is complex-how complex can helping a small child be.

They say that apathy is so popular these days, it's the only thing people care about.

41

SPACE

I have my space, you have your space, and sometimes those spaces overlap, and we have our space. At times we don't want anyone in our space, and sometimes we need someone in our space. Sometimes others encroach in our space, and we have to defend our space, and sometimes we need help defending our space, and we join our space with the space of others to create a defensive alliance of a group space. And, if we win in our cause, we take part of the loser's space for his interference with our space.

The occupants of that space are not happy and we have to send in reinforcements to quell those causing trouble. That leaves fewer of those to keep peace in our original space. To support both efforts, it is necessary to raise taxes on the inhabitants of the original space, and those who object join forces with those who object in the annexed space.

Living conditions in the annexed space is deplorable, and those are all trying to enter the original space, causing it to be overpopulated and less than desirable living conditions. So many of the original inhabitants of the original space make an alliance with those of the un-annexed part of the space that was annexed. Now the protecting forces of the original space are being outnumbered and overrun by the opposition forces.

So, it became necessary to join forces with three other neutral forces to have enough forces to defend the space. But for that commitment, the original space had to give up some space, causing overcrowding and miserable living conditions.

So representatives of all the space owners met and agreed conditions were horrible in every space, and agreed that everybody would go back to the original space conditions before all the hostilities.

But by then, many inhabitants of different spaces had been in the new spaces so long, they did not want to go back, and each such group asked for a small space to be carved out so they could live as if they were back in their original space, but be in the new space.

Now everyone was wondering what having a space now meant. All the economies of the original spaces were horrible due to the cost of defending the various spaces that they controlled, and the displaced inhabitants were even in worst condition, because they didn't exactly fit with the style of the government or the type of commerce and business in their new space.

And, now it was clear that there was not enough space for everybody. So all the leaders of the spaces got together and decided they would explore space and establish colonies in space so everyone would have their own space.

And, that is how the space program got started,

When you are at a low place in life, look at all that extra space above giving extra room to grow.

You establish the value of something when you buy, not when you sell.

I don't know what you know, and I don't know what you don't know, and I shouldn't judge you until I do.

If you are the last human someone ever sees, how they will remember mankind.

Have no fear says one from the comfort of his easy chair.

My job is to get you to see, or feel, or understand, or to care, or to do and share that information with others.

Maude: You are so un-predictable, will you ever change?

Claude: Yes.

Underneath all the cloud, confusion and façade, we are all pretty much the same.

Accountability separates good and evil people. Good people feel accountable for their actions, evil people do not.

If you just don't give a damn, there's probably not a smaller denomination you can use.

There's no rest for the wicked, and with the current political unrest, none for anyone else.

Old florist never die, they just leave.

The reason the advice from Grandma was so good was it came from a lifetime of dreaming, living, hard work, learning and loving.

Life experiences that are re-lived often are rarely forgotten. Astronauts do it out of this world.

42

MY SAY

No matter what has been said,

Nor, who it was said about,

Or, what was said,

Or, when it was said,

Or, to whom it was said,

How loudly it was said,

Or, quietly it was said,

Who heard it when it was said,

Or, who didn't hear it when it was said,

Who believed it when it was said,

Or, who did not believe it when it was said,

I really don't care,

This is my day,

And, I'll do it my way,

I'll have my say.

Why is it every time someone says, you don't say, they always say it anyways.

Stress comes when our greed wants more than our brain and body are willing to provide.

I can tell you more, but you will have to wait a while, making things up takes longer than telling the truth.

A far cry is usually within hearing distance.

No time for the wicked, doesn't necessarily mean there is for the good.

Angels have a lot of stories to tell, are the ones about you something they can repeat.

Maude: Given enough time we can make this work.

Claude: I only have one lifetime.

There are some things so good, they can only be seen by Angels.

I don't like the alternative of growing old.

For every hill to climb, there is one to struggle down.

There is much good that we don't see and will never know.

Old jailed prisoners never die, they just hang in there.

Coal miners do it underground.

Getting up on the wrong side of the bed probably means you went to bed on the wrong side.

He says, I am just one little man, I can't do anything, and he would be right.

43

MAKING IT

Make things neat,

Make life sweet,

Get things done,

Make life fun.

Don't worry whether or not you will have to slide into second base until you get on first.

It is said he is a magician with words, he call talk all day and the meaning of his words will still be invisible.

Believing is mostly a matter of faith.

Forgiveness was not a human event until God intervened.

Un-asked for advice is usually worth what you paid for it.

Since you didn't show me the courtesy of asking my advice, I will show you the courtesy of giving to you anyway.

Everyone is brave behind a locked door.

Old donkey riders never die, they just sit on their ass.

Longevity is great, too bad you have to wait so long to get it.

The people who are impatient are trampled over by those who just can't wait.

Every time you spend looking back is one minute of your future that you can't see.

Thank goodness for fear, it has saved us many a time from a do it on a dare disaster.

Hookers do it on the street.

Sometimes falling in love can be a real blow when the fall stops.

Never forget your regrets.

I can't do everything, but what I can do, I will do.

Want to find a few minutes of peace, take a nap.

There is nothing new under the sun, or above it either.

The way to win, is to hold on as long as you can, and when you can't hold on anymore, hold on some more anyway.

Laughter is a gift from God, humans are the only animal that can laugh.

Old swearers never die, they just get bleeped out.

The reason many people can't hold their tongue is its moving so fast they can't catch it.

The solution to stress is mental solitude.

If there is a reason to do it, there is probably a reason not do it, choose wisely.

The solution to you is you.

44

KAT 31

Once upon life's highway,

Traveled a lady named Kat,

She was into this,

And she was into that.

But with experience,

She put things in their place,

And got it all together,

With a smile on her face.

No more treading water,

For this lady on the go,

But it was up and over,

And away we go.

Upon this highway,

Some high standards she'll set,

Wise are those who follow,

On that you can bet.

She's developed her own way,

To get things done,

She's up and eager for new,

Challenges with each rising sun.

She puts things in high gear,

she gives them a spin,

But she likes it best,

When everybody wins.

A person on the move,

Who puts in many a mile,

But never too busy,

To stop and share a smile.

She has a unique way,

Of making everybody feel they are a part,

Probably because of those friendly vibes,

That come straight from the heart.

She has carved out her very own niche,

Through toil and sweat and yet all the while,

She did it with quiet eloquence,

And, with grace and her own style.

On Kat you can always count,

Whether it gets thick or it gets thin,

She always shoulders her corner of the load,

Right to the very end.

Set her mood down as good,

For she rarely gets mad,

And then only because the,

Underdog has been had.

You've come a long way baby,

In these few 31 years,

Moving up and out,

Overcoming all fears.

Many who are older,

Who would suggest what to do,

Would be wise to study your example,

And listen to you.

Kat, your candle is lit,

And it burns bright;

We shall hold it up to see,

As a beacon in the night.

You never cease to amaze us,

When intense times,

Your sense of humor,

Softens the drawn lines.

As a friend to all of us,

There are few to compare,

For you don't take or give,

But you share.

And someday when

This highway reaches its end,

I shall count as one of my great privileges,

To have known you, Kat, as my friend.

Celebrating the birthday of a co-worker

Not everything is for certain, and what a dull life it would be if it were.

Life is much too short, so hug and squeeze the life out of every minute.

If you repeat your mistakes, then you haven't learned anything at all.

Even a man flat broke has something to give—his time.

Sharing is proof of caring.

Some people run out of good ideas, but have an endless supply of bad ones.

The Constitution gives us many freedoms but, God gave us the gift of Choice.

Want every day to have meaning and purpose, make someone smile everyday, and make someone laugh everyday, then notice how much better your day is.

45

HELP THAT DOESN'T HURT

The way to help people in dire straits is not giving them money. With money, you make them dependent on the source of the money.

While initially, if the people are immediately hungry, you help with food and shelter, but offer a way that in time they become self-supporting through offering training in job skills, education, financial management and life skills, which are required for them to continue to receive our help.

We must manage the economy well so when they finish their training, there will be jobs for them to take. Nobody appreciates money the way people do when they earn it themselves. With the money they earn themselves, comes pride that can't be gotten anywhere else.

Giving them money only guarantees that they will remain dependent, on you, but unhappy at the same time. And, of course, by accepting your money, they lose freedom because they can keep getting the money only by following your rules. And that loss of freedom just makes them even more unhappy.

So, if they turn, under these unhappy conditions, to drugs, crime, violence, no one seems to understand why. But it would be easy to see, if people really wanted to see.

The position we would have put them in is financial slavery. No other way to say it.

And, here is the hard part, the people putting up this money which is taken from taxpayers is promised to these financial slaves for their vote. So now, the people who have given this money, have to keep giving the money, and can't stop, because no alternative is created, and people taking the money have to keep taking the money, as they have no other option, because none was created.

A very large percentage of the people receiving the money, under properly established conditions would work, would want to work, and the money that has been previously given to them could then be used for bridges and roads, cancer research, education and many good things, plus the tax earned by those working would add tot was not given to them, making a wind fall for everybody,

It appears that our elected representatives represent themselves much more than they represent us.

The true measure of a man is not what he has accumulated, but what he has given away.

Words can tell your story, so make one worth telling by choosing your words carefully.

Everyone has a choice to be neat or sloppy.

Sharing usually does not include giving someone a piece of your mind.

Old women can't die, for their work is never done.

What is the last thing you want to hear, is it hello or goodbye.

Old tight rope walkers never die, they just toe the line.

To be worthwhile, first work on the worth.

There are many reasons to grow in character, and you only need one.

Old gamblers never die, and the odds are 4 in 7.

I won't tell you again, I was trusting that you were listening the first time.

If they made a movie of your life, would it be a comedy or a tragedy, or both.

Selfishness is its own punishment.

It's a good thing our goose is cooked, or otherwise it would be us turkeys.

Old tailors never die, but it just seams that way.

All good things come to an end, but evil ones go on forever.

You are no better than the gossip you spread.

A young plant growing in the shade of its mother will never reach its full height.

The bad thing about being lonely, is you have to do it by yourself.

May all your dreams come true, and all your nightmares be forgotten.

Old drag car racers never die, they keep living on speed.

Poverty will never be eliminated until the need to greed ratio is about the same for everybody.

Just because you are related to or friends with someone, doesn't mean you have to approve of everything they do or say.

46

IN MY ROCKER

I'm just sitting here on my front porch in my rocker watching the cars go by. Where are all those cars going? Left and right, up an down, back and forth, zip, zip.

I get to thinking, maybe I'll go get a job, but then, it would probably be a boring job with a mean boss who would make my life miserable, and I will feel bad, and quit, so, no, I'll just sit here in my rocker and watch all the cars go by. Where are all those cars going anyway?

Or, maybe I'll find a girl, have a date, get to know her, get involved in a romance and ask her to marry me, but then, she probably would say no, breaking my heart, wrecking my life-no, I'll just sit here and watch all the cars go by, but where are they going?-maybe they are all lost and looking for a gas station to ask for directions.

Say, I think I will go in and have some lunch, but then, the food could be spoiled, making me sick, and the ambulance would come, and take me to the hospital and there they would pump out my stomach, and I would get 40 shots with a big square needle-no, I'll just stay here and watch all these cars go by, zip, zip. You know what, they must be in the fast lane, they all seem to be exceeding the speed limit.

I know what I'll do, I will become a minister and help save souls and give aid and comfort, but then they may find out about my mis-spent youth and run me off, leaving me sad and depressed-no, I'll just sit here and rock and watch the cars go by.

Man, there sure are a lot of cars, big ones, little ones, noisy ones, clunkers and tankers, but I still wonder where all of them are going. Maybe they are running from their wives or husbands, or their creditors.

Maybe I ought to do something, but then, I might fail, and that would bring sadness, heartbreak and despair, so here I will sit, rocking and watching, because here I won't fail-hey, I think I've got it-if I never try, then I will never fail, so I will keep rocking and watching the cars go by.

I still wonder where the heck all those cars are going.

Hate is an internal fire that first burns away your character, then your soul.

Nothing helps more than a kind word from a friend and nothing hurts more than an unkind one.

In case you haven't noticed forever is a long time.

A cold shoulder can never warm a heart.

Maude: Could you be nice to me for one day?

Claude: Is that a 12 hour day or a 24 hour day?

Want a really big puzzle, try putting all your ideas together.

Old clock makers never die, they never run out of time.

Mechanics do it with a wrench or is it a wench.

Rich people are not any more evil than poor ones.

Never look up to someone who is beneath you.

Seek the high road, the low road is usually crowded.

I think sleep is over-rated, spend 8 hours a day doing something you don't remember a single moment of.

The younger generation has only one thing the older generation doesn't – inexperience.

Money won't get you to peace of mind, but it will sure make the trip more comfortable.

Hold on to life better than you do your money.

Now-a-days when I see the naked truth, I want to put some clothes on it.

Just between friends should be nothing.

May peace be on you should be may peace be among you.

You'll realize you need to get a grip if you ever expect to get a handle on life.

Considering where I am, the best advice I can give you is don't listen to me.

Two requirements for survival—keep your head down and your mouth shut.

Respect is not given, it is earned.

Those who sit beside each other in church probably will never have face

each other with weapons outside of the church.

The tears of caring will always wash away hate.

47

I CAN'T BUT I CAN

I can't make you be a man,

But, you can lean on me until you can,

I can't stop the tears,

But, I can help with the underlying fears,

I can't guide you in the night,

But, I can always shed a little light,

I can't make your path without pain,

Because mine is the same,

I can't make you star,

But, I can help you feel you are,

I can't make love come your way,

But, I can make sure all your friends stay,

I can't make you smart,

But, I can help you understand most people aren't,

I can't make you believe in you,

But, I can show you most people do,

I can't take away the source of your strife,

But, I can show you how to live life,

I can't take away the darkness in your soul,

But, how to find the light you'll be told,

I can't make you a success,

But, I can show you how to win with excess,

I can't stop you from your broken heart,

But, I can help you on the re-start,

I can't create you a loving family,

But, until then, a poor substitute I'll be,

I can't make your dreams come true,

But, I can tell you those of most people do,

I can't make up for all the disappointment,

But, I can show you where the plan went,

I can't run the race for you,

But, I can cheer you on when you do,

I won't make of your battles light,

But, I can make sure you get a fair fight,

I can't stop the sky from falling down,

But, can show you magic in each piece found,

I can't live your life for you,

But, I can show how much better yours is when you do.

If you want time to stand still, tell your wife that you just cheated on her.

Whatever we do, whatever we try, there are no good goodbyes.

These days everybody is a critic without any critical thinking, and that is why we are in such a critical crisis.

Claude: When I was young, I was a good kid.

Maude: Too bad you had to grow up.

Being right is not necessarily the same as being good.

Repeating a mistake is punishment for having made it the first time.

The worst friend you ever had is far better than none.

If I didn't really care, you wouldn't know it.

Lying usually has its own punishment.

48

TO THE NEW MOMMY

You have dreamed of this and now,

Happily, a mommy you will soon be,

Whatever the future or the cards hold,

Whether it's one or two, or a he or she,

You will care for them, love them,

Raise them to be the best they can be,

Just as you have stood by me, and supported me,

And helped me to be the best of me.

To help support you in this great endeavor,

I will give you my sure and steady hand,

Into your future you go, one beautiful person,

And me, one happy and grateful man.

We will nurture the newborn, give much love,

We will be everything it needs in a mom and dad,

We will grow into the family we've been dreaming of,

There will be music, and our hearts will be full and glad.

The best word for you, and that is wonderful,

That my heart and brain can think of,

To my wife, Maria, may you have a wonderful

And joyous Mommyhood filled with love.

The riddle of life is no joke.

There is no beginning without an end and no end without a beginning, except for gossip.

For people or ideas, from one comes many, and from many comes one.

There are a lot of people other than Mr. Spock, who want me to live long and prosper—my creditors.

Claude: You can't talk to me like that, I'll leave.

Maude: Ok, I'll start over.

Old rifle makers never die, they just barrel along.

Old physicists never die, they just find a new dimension.

Truth is not the opposite of false, but the opposite of uncertainty.

Love can bring joy, but also pain.

The success of many a man can be traced back to the love of a good woman.

49

THE MOTIVATOR

_____

I was there to help, it was at their request,

I thought I could do it, I would do my best.

There were many of them in the big room that day,

And they came from far and near to hear what I had to say.

They wanted to be pushed, and each one of them be lifted up,

And, I could tell by listening, there was little in their cup,

I heard tales of bad things, and times ever so rough,

Just barely getting by was the norm, and life was very tough.

How all the business was bad, and the usual sales were sadly down,

And, how many of them, would probably have to leave town,

My heart was so heavy, listening to their sad tale of woes,

Today I would have to be good, I would need to be on my toes.

So, I started out with the old story, of the man who was always late,

And, almost always missed everything, every meeting and every date,

I don't squander my time, he said as he pondered and he thought,

Then he went out, and a shiny new clock he bought.

But, that didn't help at all, so he so soon found out,

Now, he was really perplexed, and began to mope and pout,

I'm losing several precious minutes, every single hour or so,

And, he asked himself, just where do all those minutes go.

Maybe just run away somewhere, or they just sneak off and hide,

Because where they were, they didn't like and could not abide,

So, they go somewhere, maybe somewhere between now and then,

Yes, he said, that's where they go, but I just can't say exactly when.

And, that's when he realized, to his amazement, and, he, in fact did find,

That the time he had forever lost, was lost in the time of his behind,

That's when he said no, I'll never again lose time on the clock bands,

Because, I'll reach and grab it, and take it with me with both hands,

We, then talked together, about how to set goals and achieve,

And with feeling, moved on to hope and how to make ourselves believe,

We developed simple plans that were real, and that they could actually do,

A plan that provided for achievement, and plans of life enrichment too.

A plan with immediate rewards, and those for times later, also,

With inherent and instructive feedback, and self-correcting to make it so,

Work hard, work smart, be firm, be frugal and save your pay,

And invest cautiously and carefully, and wisely along the way.

Also, to take a minute or two, and smell a rose once in a while,

Lend a hand when you can, be thankful and grateful and smile,

And, they were eager with smiles, joyous and standing and ready to go.

Off to work was their thought, to slay a couple of dragons or so.

But, there was something I could see, and I could tell it was on their mind,

The side glances and the looking down, and the looking behind,

What was it that was so troubling, causing the hesitation, the stall,

Whatever it was, was infecting, and causing the hesitation in them all.

What is this thing that has them stopped, on which they did need to agree,

I needed to search through my mind, weave a little magic to set them free,

For answers I reached deep in my soul, and struggled hard in my brain,

And, so hard and deep, I thought perhaps I would go insane.

These people are successful, with what they brought forward in time,

So, it must be something, they carelessly or thoughtlessly left behind,

Something they knew, or should have known or have met,

I could tell right then, they left something behind they did regret.

They probably hurt, insulted or belittled, someone along the way,

And, in their eager climb to success, that's the way it would stay,

But, the story is now known, and there it should not and cannot end,

So, I told them that they must, do whatever they must, to make amend,

They must go back to the one person, to whom they caused the pain,

And, with heart in hand, beg for forgiveness and be free again,

I knew then that I was done, I had done everything I could,

And, I saw in their eyes, that they would do what they should.

And there was loud applause, but I could not hear it then,

But, I knew as I left the room, everyone there had become a friend,

And, I believed, that everything was all right as I reached the back door,

For, as I looked in amazement, everyone there, was kneeling on the floor.

Dancers do it on the floor.

You can't measure love by the length of a dollar bill.

Want to have no more wars, make the politicians be the first people called into the military when a war is started.

Want to make sure that only the truly guilty are punished, make the judge and the prosecutor serve the balance of the sentence, of a defendant who is found innocent after serving part of a sentence.

Old pool players never die, they just put their balls in a pocket.

If you talk enough, you may stumble around and finally say something.

If they make toilet paper any thinner or more narrow, it won't be any good to wipe your nose and certainly not to wipe anything else.

Any human can monkey around better than any monkey can.

Tears are like wash day, they wash the dirty out.

If there is an entrance, where is the outrance?

Why was he called a cowboy, he rode a horse, should've been called a horse boy, he didn't ride the cows.

Maude: How come you won't love me forever and forever?

Claude: Because one forever is all I've got.

If the best you can do is be in the mediocre mellow middle, then be the best at it you can be.

50

RHYME

I knew there would come a time,

When nothing I wrote seemed to rhyme

Words were tools of my trade,

And everyday words of wisdom and wit I made.

I wrote words of kindness and feeling of glad,

And, words of regret and feeling sad,

I gave them words for a wistful goodbye

And, words to put a tear in their eye.

Words of comfort when losing someone,

And words of hope for those who have none,

To those who have had success past them by,

I give words of hope for another try.

And, to those who found love and lost

Encouragement to try again at all cost,

All my words were always true,

With words of comfort for me and you.

My words came to me easy and quick,

And, those words required no anguish or trick,

Words kept coming from whence I could not tell,

Now, they don't come at all, or not so well.

The words just don't come around,

And, I am lost and feeling really down,

I used to have words that gave a clue,

On ideas of things useful to me and you.

I'm about ready to give up and out,

And, I know exactly what I'm talking about,

If I don't get a manuscript to the publisher for real,

I may be missing many a meal.

I don't know exactly what to tell you,

And, I don't exactly know what I plan to do,

I'm just going in circles, trying to find a rhyme,

But, seems that I am just wasting my time.

And, no matter what grammar gymnastics I do or say,

With clutter in my head, I'm the one in my way,

Those words, beautiful words, where have they gone,

All that's left are words that's been stripped to the bone.

I could look, and pray and then look some more,

There just isn't anything anywhere like a rhyming store,

And, I'm not sure it's worth the look and time,

Because, I just can't get the damned things to rhyme.

Doing something way out of the norm will get you noticed, and in some cases can get you jailed.

There is an easy way to balance the budget, just make the politicians personally liable for the over budget spending.

It takes a person of great character who will manage your assets as well as he does his own.

Old concrete workers never die, they just cement their future.

Old bakers never die, they just continue to show their buns.

Things come and go, especially time.

Self-centered people believe that everything should point to them except their mistakes.

Every sentence that has the word can't should end with the word yet.

51

MATTERS OF THE HEART

Butter beans are good for the heart,

The more you eat, the more you fart,

The more you fart, the better you feel,

So eat butter beans every meal.

You can't find the answer if you don't know the question.

Maude: How many women have you slept with before me?

Claude: With those women, I didn't sleep.

Old train workers never die, they just make tracks.

Scotsmen do it in their kilts.

They say life will make you humble, and humble will make you tall, right now, I think I'm up to about 10 feet.

You heart can lead your brain to the right choice.

Just because you lost yesterday, doesn't mean you can't win today.

Peace and prosperity—sure would be nice to get those two together someday.

If you can't find any other reason to continue to climb, then, do it because you're just too damned stubborn to quit.

The friend most likely to offer their life to save yours is a spouse.

Old fisherman never die, but that story is a little fishy.

Getting the short end of the stick is not so bad if that is where the money is.

After a serious mistake, don't look in the mirror, you already know what a failure looks like.

Trying to do the right thing means you have not done it.

At the end of the list of all the things you didn't do, add the word, yet.

In life, hope for the best, look for the good, expect the worst, and you will never be disappointed.

You don't have to be contrary to make a difference.

Believe only what you see, and pray you'll see enough to believe.

If you have too many choices and each seems to have about the same value, think each one through to the end considering all the intended and un-intended consequences, and see what you have left.

They said love conquers all, I gave love, and she conquered me.

Sometimes things turn out wrong after the best planning and effort, accept it, learn what you can from it, and move on.

You rarely get a second first chance, so make the first one good.

Sometimes your mouth is as big as your pride.

Old steel workers never die, they just forge on.

Old beer barrel makers never die, they just stave it off.

Maude: Did you love me at first sight?

Claude: Yes, but that was before I got my glasses.

Finding the meaning doesn't necessarily reveal purpose.

Will we be remembered by those who come after as much as those who came before.

If them are fighting words is all it takes for you to fight you are gonna have a lot of broken bones in your life.

First moron: They say you can't get to heaven in a golden chariot.

Second moron: Probably a wooden one won't work either.

If you are waiting for good things to come to you, don't hold your breath.

If you try hard enough, making believe can become making real.

It takes a lot of study for one to become studious.

52

LITTLE

Little ideas,

Little ways,

Little of heart,

And, Little stays.

We were going to get a magician to do his disappearing act for us, but we can't find him.

Many a war has been fought over peace.

We have been dividing ever since the first one-celled protoplasm, but considering some of the latest results, probably time for that to end.

Old soda drinkers never die, they just fizzle out.

You can be as happy as you want to be.

Claude: If you didn't nag so much, we could have a conversation.

Maude: If I didn't nag, there would be no nothing to talk about.

It's gonna take a long time to pay off all of my creditors, I guess that's why they keep sending me vitamins.

They said give everybody your love, I tried, but there were many who violently objected.

One thing that doubters never run out of is doubt.

We would be able to see more of ourselves, if we could just stop looking in the mirror.

Sometimes the best thing we can do is nothing.

I can't always be there for you, for sometimes I have to be there for me.

It's better to have doubts than to think you know everything.

Sometimes the only thing you can do is just hold on, and sometimes it's the best thing you can do.

There is a difference between being brave and being stupid.

Sometimes, helping someone is no more than just getting out of the way.

With no hills to climb, you soon forget how to climb.

If you don't look up, it's hard to find a reason to go up.

Of all the gifts given to us, the one right after life is laughter.

Old atheists never die, they have nowhere to go.

Old black ravens never die, they just live never-more.

No one knows what goes on in the bedroom between a husband and wife, but, if they have a truck load of kids you probably have a pretty good idea.

All farts never die, they just run out of gas.

Dumb: They say that tomorrow never comes.

Dumber: Oh, it will definitely come if you have a bad hangover.

The only thing a small child understands is the time from his or her parents, even time while being disciplined is desired over no time, and all the gifts in the world will not make up for the lack of it.

If you don't stand up for the things that are right, you may have to sit through years of things that are wrong.

People who use mind altering drugs do so they say to escape. What do they escape? Responsibility, in other words, they become worthless to others and to themselves and have no reason to live except to continue to be worthless.

First moron: Why is the number 11 relaxing?

Second moron: Because it is past tense.

We describe love in a hundred ways and wonder which one is right-newsflash-they all are.

Old vegetarians never die, they just finally meat up.

The way to take sex is any way you can get it, legally, of course.

First moron: Why do they call him Uncle Sam?

Second moron: He's supposed to be that rich uncle who gives away money—he is and does; our money.

Never trust a man who can talk faster than you can think.

53

THIS LITTLE POEM

This little poem I'm trying to write,

Everyday, morning, noon and night,

I use all my effort, and all my skill,

All my might muster and will.

It seems no matter how I try,

It won't work and I am ready to cry

It's so even though and even when,

I make up a word every now and then.

But, even with all the effort and all this time

The blasted thing still just won't rhyme.

Look inside if you need courage, it's in there somewhere.

Sometimes when I don't know what to do, I have to feel my way along.

Maude: I want to talk to you about a drinking problem.

Claude: Yours or mine.

If it's the last thing you can do, then don't do it for me.

By your thoughts and deeds you can die long before you stop breathing.

If you can't offer a kind word, then stay quite.

On life's road, the junctions have no signs, but never mind, whether long or short, hard or easy, every road, with determination and patience leads to somewhere.

At 21, it's fun in the sun; at 31, it's job advancement, stress and mortgages; at 41, it's mid-life crisis, job enrichment, plans for retirement, suburbs, SUV's and PTA; at 51 it's bridgework, college tuition, second mortgage, more saving for retirement; at 61, where did the time go?

I'm not procrastinating; I am just waiting for just the right opportunity.

If all your enemies became friends, what would you fight for.

There is only one difference between an enemy and a friend—you.

You can get behind two years in sex and catch up in 5 minutes.

If you really believe in being tolerant, then show it by being quiet.

The reason so many people are lost, they go around circles stumbling over the same obstacles, what they should do is go in a straight line and sooner or later they will get somewhere.

Candy makers do it with sticky fingers.

Old song writers never die, for the song never ends.

If you don't think there are limits, just ask those teenage boys how far they got on their first date.

Limits are what makes society have order, without them there would only be anarchy and chaos.

Maude: Neither of us has ever drank.

Claude: Looks like at least one of us has to start.

Old chimney sweeps never die, they can't find anything that soots them.

Want to make sure delinquent fathers pay their child support, sentence them not to jail where they watch TV and play cards, but to a work farm, where they make products for sale, and if they don't work, they don't eat, and all the profit they generate goes for child support, and after 12 months see if they are ready to pay what they are required, voluntarily.

Going faster than your natural speed in anything is dangerous.

The only time an airplane is dangerous is during descent.

It is said that man cannot live by bread alone, unless its sweet rolls, then maybe.

Too bad the greed exceeds the need.

It's not a chance, if you stay on the floor, you have to dance.

Just because you are poor doesn't mean you have to be poor in spirit.

They said I should gamble. I told them not a chance.

How well a young man turns out, depends on his relationship with his mother, and how well a young lady turns out, depends on her relationship with her father.

The good thing about hope is it continues even when there is no reason to.

54

POCAHONTAS
THE SONG

He was a stranger,

Here in her world,

She was a lonely,

Indian Girl.

It was just magic,

Indian maid,

A red haired stranger,

Magic they made

Lost in her beauty,

She is his charms,

Both found a new love,

Her in his arms.

The stranger set sail

Promises to keep,

She stayed in her world,

Alone she would sleep

She sought for love,

He sought for fame,

They sought together

Both found the same.

Everyone should have 5 persons that they can name as a mentor or coach who had or is having a major positive effect in their life and be able to say how.

There have been books written about, poems written about, songs sung about, the good times, those times which involved family, friends, communities, pride, food, celebrations and honor, and my wish to you is may most of your times be good times.

This is a land of fisherman, everybody is fishing for something, money, fame, friends, love, salvation, opportunity, entertainment, forgiveness, peace, and a few are actually fishing for fish.

May your beliefs be as strong as those of a small child.

Life is filled with hard choices, may you develop the ability to make wise ones, and the fortitude to live with the results afterward.

Like most people, I am not a lot, but what little I do have, I am going to use wisely.

Respect is what you earn as you are doing, honor is what is awarded to you after what you have finished.

Claude: Why can't you cook like my mother?

Maude: I don't know how your mother cooks.

Never send a boy to a man's fight, for you may get back neither a victory no the boy.

Old magicians never die, but that might just be an illusion.

Babies do it in their diapers.

Maude: You don't tell me you love me anymore.

Claude: Yeah, it's about the same.

Want to know the secret of how to have a wonderful life, start doing good, and keep doing good, and it will come to you.

I don't need to relieve the past, one time of all that is enough.

Maude: Do you have an answer for all my questions?

Claude: No, but I will after you ask them.

You never miss what you never had.

It may be a long way to the bottom of the well, but that is where the water is.

One thing that will never desert you, your shadow.

Many people want to tell a story, but first they have to have a story to tell.

55

GEOMETRY

Once a little triangle was dangling at an angle,

He was happy and grinned with a big arc smile

And, with enthusiasm, he jumped over the square root,

Skipped across the hypotenuse, fell and busted his acute.

There he hung, with his right angle down,

While his angle opposite was swinging around,

He reached for a perpendicular,

Slipped and scraped his circular.

He was determined to set his adjacent upright,

So he pushed a radian around with all his might,

And, made a line from a point to the right,

Then used the vertical to pull the points in tight.

Then pivoting from his fulcrum to his base,

His isosceles sides dropped into place,

With this much success, he gave a big parallel,

Sat on his focal point and rested a spell.

Then reflecting, while leaning against a vertical plane,

And also, feeling somewhat rather sad,

He thought I wonder what has happened here?

All my lines are crossed really bad.

I've lost all the points that touch,

I'm just not what I used to be,

He leaned against the opposite, and opened his arc

And let all his pent-up tangents go free.

I started out hanging just for fun.

Now look what has happened and what I've done,

I think my point has become dull,

I don't think I will ever be an equilateral.

Being a little triangle is just no use,

And tho' I don't think it's anything like fair,

Having to always be obtuse,

Guess I'll have to settle for being a little square.

Always let an infant crawl, if you don't, the baby will grow up to be clumsy.

Just so you'll know, the lost generation still hasn't been found.

Too many directions can cause one to become lost.

I'm not sorry I said it, because I had no evil intent, I am sorry you had an evil intent that caused you to take it the wrong way.

Deep water runs slow and deep societal changes likewise move slow.

Maude: I never want to see you again.

Claude: You can start by looking the other way.

Billiard players often rack up more than their balls, just make sure they don't rack yours up.

Low and mean is more about character than elevation.

Old arsonist never die, they just flame-out.

Foresters do it in the woods.

Shallow water comes and goes quickly, just as shallow human character.

The only reason you have things worth holding on to is someone held on to them before you.

The last dance usually doesn't end the night.

There's always a storm brewing somewhere in almost everything.

A smile is medicine for the heart.

If there was ever a good time to wonder about things, this is it.

I stay awake many a night wondering why I can't sleep.

If you are always looking down, you will never see the glorious sun, nor the beautiful blue sky, and you will miss much beauty.

If I have to count to 10 again to keep from getting mad, I'm gonna be really angry.

Many people spend a major portion of their lives trying to find something they hate more than themselves.

Squeezing the devil out of a baby is not the way to show him love.

A pause in your talk or presentation at the right place and correct length can draw your audience in better than your words, because the audience fills in the blanks with their own imagination.

Sometimes the best way to a person's brain is through his emotions.

Laughter can open your listener's heart and his brain.

Live your life so that those who come after you can learn from you as much as you did from those who came before you.

Being in a pickle usually doesn't happen in a jar.

Honesty in your heart can be heard in your voice.

Choosing whether life is good or life is bad, each has a different path and each leads to a different ending.

56

TOLERANCE

Being tolerant means we will recognize those we believe inferior to us in some way, otherwise there is nothing to tolerate, but having identified that difference, we will tolerate that difference and treat that person or group as equal, while still recognizing a difference. That is, tolerate them.

What we should be doing is seeing no difference, so there is nothing to tolerate. As long as there are people or groups who preach tolerance, while at the same time always recognizing and treating that person or group as being different then tolerance will be required, which means the person or group will be recognized as different and regardless of all the tolerance talk, the person or group will always be treated differently, because the tolerant talking people have isolated the tolerated people and put them into a box or a cage with their rhetoric, and pointing to them and saying those are the people who (the group) are being discriminated against. It should be clear, that any people who are identified as a group and given labels will have to be tolerated.

And to events where people of the tolerated group have been hurt emotionally or physically by a person, law enforcement or the government, it should and must not happen, not because the person is one of a tolerated group, but because it should not happen to any person. The same rules applies to everybody whether they are in the tolerated group or not, and the law must, absolutely must, be applied equally as if there were no groups, and except for a few lunatics, this is what all rational and reasonable people want.

Any time groups develop, each tries to pull center mass in its direction. There should be no center mass. Every individual and his or her actions need to be treated as one person judged individually and fairly. When they are put in a group, unfortunately part of how they are treated and judged is influenced by how the group is viewed. That is unfair to the person and to the socio-economic and judicial system.

This is America, and everyone has a right to live without being branded into a group or identified as one of a group, so his life and his behavior is judged by him and his actions, and his alone, and not be tainted by some artificial group to which he has been assigned, and in many cases without his permission.

To all the self-appointed spokes-people, you keep identifying people in groups, so, as you say, to help them. What you are doing is permanently making them susceptible to abuse by keeping them locked in a group just as if they were in jail.

Please, give them a chance to stand as one and be judged as one. It is their right. We are not a nation of groups, we are a nation of people with individual rights from God, guaranteed by the Constitution.

I pray for the day when we all have just one label: American.

Why is it every time someone says give me a second, they always take at least a minute.

A whiner just wants someone to solve his problem.

Intuition is the uncanny ability to rightfully forecast the future, with so little information that logically it can't be done.

There are always more reasons than answers.

Maude: I don't appreciate you going off and leaving me standing at the store.

Claude: Why didn't you just sit down.

If you could see into the future just one-thousandth of a second, in a week you could change the world, and anyway, how do we know that some people can't.

If one plus one didn't equal three, there would be no people on earth.

Farmers do it in a barn.

When it comes to jumping into the game, just take your best shot, the perfect time may never come.

Never ask for what you are not willing to give.

The most racist thing you can do is call someone else racist.

The correct response to being called a racists, is to say, yes, I am a member of the human race, you, for some reason have been left out.

Sometimes running from pillar to post can bring down the house.

If there are many good reasons to do something, that means you should have already done it.

They say no good deed goes unpunished and probably no bad ones either.

I may not be all you are, but I can be all that I am.

If you've never had an original thought before, don't try to make me think you have one now.

Don't be the kind of father who has to tell his son-don't be like me.

They say, make love, not war, I'm not so sure, the world is already over-populated.

Someday, someway, somehow we are going to make it-so hang in there.

With sex, for any more than you can stand, you may have to lie down.

Music can give your heart wings.

While others are working out, I'm figuring how I can work my way in.

It's not good to be not wanted, unless it's in reference to the sheriff.

If you go back to your roots, don't be surprised to find they have all sprouted.

Saving means giving up a want for a need.

A lamb should never make an alliance with a wolf, for one day the wolf may be a little extra hungry.

Sometimes your mind is like a magician, it will play tricks on you.

The call of the wild can happen in the city as well as the jungle.

It's never too late to show courage.

A little bit more works well until there is no more.

If you never reach, you never get.

If you dance with the devil, expect to get burned.

Being brave and being stupid are entirely two different things.

All the crazy, stupid little things we do will one day add up to a giant blunder.

If I knew which direction to go, I could face my future.

All it takes to end the darkness is for one person to light a candle.

Everybody has a right to have rights, and it's only right.

We are all completely unique, but only to the extent that we are all uniquely the same.

Having faith sometimes means accepting the inevitable.

Fisherman do it in the ocean.

Old sky divers never die, they just chute along.

First moron: You said that a rooster woke you up every morning what did you do?

Second moron: Since my wife had locked me out, I moved from the chicken house to the dog house.

Even one voice against tyranny can be heard.

They say there is a reason for everything, and not all of them are good.

Most of our dreams are dependent on other people, so be nice to everybody.

They said give it your all, I did, and they took it.

Old garbage men never die, they just waste-a-way.

If you can't see the whole picture, it's because you are picking favorites.

57

HOW IT WORKS OUT

I don't need anyone, I'm my own man,

I go where my heart leads and make my own plan,

I'm not pulled off course by what others say,

I follow my own vision and do it my way.

Some with quite voices much advice they gave,

Others were loud and would rant and rave,

I looked inside and followed the direction from me,

And, in none of my decisions was there a we.

So, I moved on with this plan for one,

Following my view for what had to be done,

I worked long on this self-directed plan of mine,

And, it never, ever worked out, any of the time.

We all have a choice, we can extend to the world a hand or a fist.

You will treasure the things most that you earn.

The best way to get good friends is to be one.

Going down a slippery slope is a one-way trip.

The solution to stress is mental solitude.

It would be a great world if those who consumed were those who produced.

It is usually a very hard bed when you have to sleep-on-it.

We should all take a lesson from the wood cutter and just let the chips fall where they may.

If you are going through a divorce, you can prove you never loved the other person at all by continuing to hate them, and , thereby proving the only person you ever loved was yourself.

A child growing up in a home where Mom and Dad hate each other will never learn how to love, only how to hate.

You prove your depth of human character not when things are easy, but when they are hard.

You can be smart enough to break the rules and get away with it, but that does not prove that you are smart.

There are many four letter words that we should not say, but love is not one of them

While we shouldn't use four letter words, but in those moments where we are frustrated beyond words, it feels so damn good to use one of them.

You cannot convince the world what a good Christian you are by showing them how humble and sad you are for the sin of the world, and you would punish yourself is necessary. If we have learned nothing else from the life of Christ, Christians should be filled with joy, laughter, dance and song, for the abundant life is yours for free.

There are only two differences between the truth and a lie, 1. The facts, and 2. The way we interpret the facts.

Maude: This is the end, I can't say it any other way.

Claude: How about goodbye?

The last thing you should do every day is take a mental assessment of your day.

You can run many races and not be first in any of them, but you can still score enough to be overall winner, which shows there are many ways to win.

Thinking things through will sometimes allow you to see a result bad enough to terminate the plan.

Never allow your feelings or emotion to overrule your calculated sober judgment.

However, in choosing a life partner, a calculated sober judgment would have you choose a friend, but which choice is void of romantic chemistry, which of course will doom the relationship. Choosing a life partner is all about feelings and emotion and sometimes it works and sometimes not, but when it does, it can be the grandest thing in your life

Unfortunately, getting the goods on someone usually does not mean supplying them with clothes.

A smile is an indication of a moment of inner peace.

THE END

THANKS AND WISHES

Thanks for taking a look,

And, reading my crazy little book.

I hope it brought some joy to you,

And, made you smile a time or two.

Now, here is my wish for you.

May your nights be quiet and cool,

Your days be sunny, but not hot,

May your friends be many,

And, there be few who are not.

Dance like no one is watching you,

And, sing like no one is listening, too,

May you live the best life you can,

And, your life show the goodness of Man,

That it be sheltered in His Plan,

While He holds you safely in His Hand.

ABOUT THE AUTHOR

Cody Wayne Foote lives in east central Alabama with his wife, Maria.

He is and has been an engineer, a lawyer, a mediator, arbitrator, a jeweler, a designer and builder of homes and a ballroom and line dance instructor.

His message to himself every day is: In your endeavor to find fairness and justice for all, may you never tire.

The author's next book, which is being written, will be entitled: *Stories I Can't Forget* (True Stories) – which is planned for distribution, hopefully, in 2021.

You may reach him at codywaynefoote@gmail.com

DEDICATION

This book is dedicated to my Wife, Maria.

ACKNOWLEDGEMENTS

I thank Laura McGarvey for her expert help in typing and organizing the manuscript for this book.

I thank all the people who have influenced my life in a positive way to give me the motivation to write this book. There are too many to list here, but many thanks to you all.

PROLOGUE

At last sighting, Maude and Claude were still together.